HOW **<u>NOT</u>** TO

KILL YOUR

KIDS BEFORE

THEY TURN 18

TONYA E. JOYNER

How NOT to Kill Your Kids Before They Turn 18

Scripture quotations marked KJV are from the King James Version of the Bible.

Scripture quotations marked The Message Bible are taken from *The Message*. Copyright © 1993, 1994, 1995, 1996, 2000, 2001, 2002. Used by permission of NavPress Publishing Group.

Published in the United States of America

ISBN-13: 978-1492795674
ISBN-10: 1492795674

DEDICATION

This book is dedicated to my three favorite little people-my children. You've made parenthood a wonderful & adventurous event & you always keep me laughing! I'm so grateful for the blessing of being your Mom & pray that in fifteen to thirty years when you have kids of your own, you'll have this book around even if I'm not. I love you dearly & am so proud of you!

~Mommy

This book is also dedicated to "those crazy old people"-my parents. I could never ask for better role models of what works & what doesn't! You've been the best parents ever & I thank you for all of the time, effort & cash you've poured into our lives. I appreciate all of the sacrifices you have made for me & I hope you are proud of what I've accomplished. I love you!

~Little Rabbit Foo Foo

Finally, to my husband, I want to express my sincere love and adoration. You are my complete opposite & perfect match! I am so glad God gave us kids. It allows me to experience all of your greatness, compassion & love through 3 other mini versions of you! I love you endlessly & thank you for your encouragement, nudges & irritating tips that were gold! Thank you so much for loving me just as I am.

~Queen

CONTENTS

Preface   i

1 Parenting Basics   1

2 Keep It Together-Organization   16

3 Herding the Sheep (Putting a System in Place)   26

4 Communication and Disagreements   33

5 Kid Stuff-Stuff Kids Just Do (Behavior   50
   Modification)

6 Life Preservers-Tips for Other Hot Topics   76

7 Teens and Tweens   96

PREFACE

The funny thing I've found about parenting is that my parents were much wiser than I originally thought. At the beginning phases of creating this book, I still considered my parents to be a bit cuckoo. Of course, most kids think their parents are "crazy old people". By the time I got to the end of writing this book, I had realized that nothing was wrong with them. They were just doing what they thought was the best thing at that given moment. As parents, what are we trying to constantly figure out? The best thing to do for the long term and for the moment!

So, let's get one thing out of the way the legal stuff. Let me start by giving a disclaimer:

I am <u>NOT</u> a psychologist, therapist, counselor, or licensed professional in this area. I'm a person who has kids, works with kids, teaches kids, has helped others raise their kids, and has taken notes on how people raise their kids. I've seen what works and what doesn't.

This book is a collection of facts, opinions, and ideas for parents. They are not guaranteed to work (there is no hard and fast rule for parenting besides love)!

This book is intended to give you insight and inspiration on how to deal with common issues in the parent-child relationship. It's for use at your own discretion and your own risk.

This book is for parents who need new ways to approach a problem; there are lots of ways in this book.

Long story short, I hope you find a method included in the pages of this book that helps you raise your child, but there's a chance (pretty slim if you ask me) that <u>none</u> of the ideas mentioned work. Keep in mind; all kids are different. What works wonders for one may not work at all for another.

So why did I write this book? I'm a former public school teacher and college professor who has taught children and adults math from 6th grade up. I've watched children grow up and saw what parenting choices could cause because I've taught the same child in 6th grade, in high school, and again in college. I've mentored and monitored quite a few children from child to adult. I've seen them grow and prosper. I've seen them regress and decline. As a mom and a teacher, I want to pass on priceless information (in plain English) that may make all the difference in raising your child. I can't say it'll all work out perfectly or that it'll work out overnight, but I can give you the hope of having tools that may help you navigate some of the waters of parenthood.

1 PARENTING BASICS

A Solid Foundation

Train up a child in the way they should go, and when they are old, they shall not depart from it. Proverbs 22:6 KJV

When you're a parent, you are a teacher, mentor, coach, instructor, motivator, and more. It takes dedication and tenacity. You may want seasons of parenthood to end (potty training and puberty come to mind), but value and cherish each and every day. You are not only teaching but learning. You do have the inside track, though. They *are* yours. Anything you did as a child has a chance of repeating. You can take that either way. If you're good at something, they may be too. You just need to make opportunities for them to express it. If you are horrible at something, there's a possibility they may be too. If you made your parents climb the walls or if you were a perfect angel, they may be too. However, don't be upset if they're not just like you. They're not supposed to be!

Here's an example. My dad can draw <u>anything,</u> and it'll be absolutely flawless. I mean, he could draw a person so accurately it looks like it should be breathing! He can also paint, build, or fix just about anything on earth. I can't draw that well, and I'm not as great at fixing things. I can design, visualize, redecorate, and organize like nobody's business. As a child, I was sad I couldn't do the things my dad could do. I had to learn that our skill sets just aren't the same, and that's ok. I've found <u>me</u> and am sticking with being the best <u>me</u> (with room for error). As a parent, I help my kids find who they are and not to knock themselves because they're not like me or someone else. They were designed by God to be different. Every person is a completely different reflection of God, and we must nurture that.

Finally, take an active role. Some parents solve problems by giving their child their way to "keep the peace". Giving in when it's not good for them is not good at all. You can do this by avoiding tough conversations, not making the tough decisions, or just not being there at all. Other methods include throwing money at them, downplaying their concerns, or brushing them off. This is not the way of having a solid, tangible relationship. However, it just creates more problems later-entitlement (a spoiled brat) or a child who does bigger and grander antics in order to get their parents' attention. I'm so weary of hearing about children who took their own lives because they felt no one cared about them. Let your kids know you're involved and that you care. If you're going to give in to keep the peace, they should clearly understand that it's you forgiving an offense and moving on for the better of all, not that you are avoiding your parental role.

You Are a Role Model

Most people are visual learners. If that's the case, this explains one very evident truth: they'll do what they see long before they do what you say. <u>Be</u> what you want to see from them! Recently, I had a discussion with a colleague about my daughter. My daughter mimics almost everything I say, wear, and do. If I was on my laptop, she pretended to work on one (we eventually got her one that was age-appropriate). When I started writing my first book, she was making her own books left and right. She even copies my fashion sense! So, the light bulb came on that the short shorts, visible bra straps, and other traits I don't want her to emulate cannot be seen in or on me. Of course, be reasonable. Take time to talk about why we wear this in the house, not outside. Same goes for my sons. They'll be looking for a wife or girlfriend at some point, and I want them to look for a woman who respects herself. So now is the time to tighten up my image even more. Start when they're young. If they're not young and you're just starting, it's still not too late. You can open a great door for communication by explaining to them why you're changing what you do, say or wear.

Be Patient and Forgiving

Oh my goodness. I remember from the age of about 10 to 16, my dad bought my mom a crystal pitcher. And every year, without fail, I broke it! I didn't do it on purpose (I was a pretty good kid for the most part), but I was in those clumsy years. I would drop it on the way to fill it, on the way to the dining room table, on the way to put it away, or on the way to wash it. It was ridiculous! Finally, my dad just stopped buying them. As a parent, I would have just forbidden me to touch them, but hey, it was not my house! Anyway, the interesting thing is, I never remember my mom yelling at me about it. I don't have that testimony about my dad. But my mom helped me clean it up and comforted me when I cried about what I'd done. She was really patient with me. I don't know why. I would have killed me a long time ago!

Why am I saying all this? It's because kids will be kids. They'll take your stuff, break your stuff, sneak your stuff, use your stuff without permission, eat your food, get stuff all sticky with the food they stole from you and have the nerve to lie about it, not say sorry and do it again later in the same day! They're kids. They mess up. Hopefully, you'll teach them to be kind, and they'll apologize or try to make it right.

Let me tell you a funny story. I live in a house with three little people who will find our adult clothes in their clean clothes and not return them. There have been months we couldn't find matching socks (puts us in a terrific mood right before church). We've hunted for shirts that we <u>know</u> we just washed. One time my favorite black capri pants went missing for almost two months. I thought I'd given them away! I had finally given up on them when my 12-year-old son (who I'd asked to look in his room for them countless times), comes downstairs and with an unbelievably innocent face says, "Mommy, are these yours? I found them in my room." I went off! For about three days!! I'll admit it. I'm not perfect. However, after I went off, nothing else of mine has gone missing. God help their daddy.

Have a Longevity Outlook (Long Term Perspective)

Parents (moms especially) sometimes get upset over small, insignificant things. I'm just being real. Stuff like flipping out over a dirty counter, but not acknowledging the beautiful art made for me by the child who made the mess. Yes, I've done it. Our pastor calls it "majoring in the minors". We've been programmed to strive for continual perfection in every area by our society. Instead, we should focus on significant things of all sizes. "Mommy look what I did!", "Dad, will you come to my game?", or "Can I invite my friends over?" are all doors of opportunity. These doors are ways to support and be an active part of your child's life. It will also increase and widen the body of their experiences. When we don't walk through these open doors, we increase the chances of those doors being shut to us. Even more, we root importance and acceptance issues, not to mention feelings of isolation when we aren't there for our kids. That's when they'll recruit other people (who don't always mean them well) to enter into their vulnerable places. When those opportunities to engage with your children arise, act on them. It'll deter unwanted situations in their future.

Team Mindset

If you have a team, use it. If you don't have a team, get one. One of the biggest errors parents can make is to "cocoon" their kids. Kids who aren't allowed to have experiences that cause bonding and social growth can become stunted. Be sure to find safe methods for them to spend time with their peers. Some examples are playdates, sleepovers, parties, kids conferences, ministry trips, and clubs. If you don't allow your kids to engage, they'll end up using you as their outlet, and you'll quickly wear out. For example, I remember when my daughter went to school for the first time. When the weekend came, she expected me to play with her like the 18 people she'd played with all day. I'd play, but goodness, after about the second hour, I started to wind down and wear out! Also, as a parent, you know there are other things that must be done. So eventually I'd spend time with her doing some fun stuff and some "come help Mommy" stuff. But we also ended up setting up play dates. They were real lifesavers!

So, how to find a team? They're most likely already within your reach. There are many parts to the team.

Family, friends, neighbors, and even strangers should be a part of your team. Yes, strangers. They can be a great learning tool. My kids have learned a ton from observing strangers. They've seen examples of how to be kind, how to be a servant to others, the results of being cruel, how important it is to practice good hygiene, and many other things. Some lessons are hilarious, while some are very serious.

Once, after coming home from church, we took a route that I despise. Since my husband was driving, I didn't have a choice. As we went down the street, we saw two grown women fighting in the parking lot of a business, dangerously close to traffic. There were about six people gathered around them, egging them on. Obviously, we had to have a family discussion about what we all saw. My oldest wanted to stop and help. My husband let our children know that if they weren't with us, we most likely would have stopped, but their safety was our first priority. We did see someone across the street on the phone and assumed they were calling the police).

My kids learned some important things about human nature that day. They learned how not to behave in public and how not treat people (those former lessons on keeping your hands to yourself and not instigating were surely solidified in their minds). They learned when it's appropriate to stop and help, when to call for help and when to just pray for help. Sometimes you should do all of the above! So when crazy things occur right in front of them, don't ignore it or downplay it. Take the opportunity to try to explain it. If you don't know, don't be afraid to say so. It teaches them that parents don't always have the answers and that it's ok for them to not always have the answers. They also learned to listen to their mommy when she says **_not_** to do something!

Ok, so back to the team concept. On your team, you should have several components (some business models have this structure). I highly suggest you check out the construct from Jessica Hagy, where she has outlined a list of 6 people you must have on your team! It's excellent!

Consistent

Say what you mean, mean what you say and do what you say you're going to do! Do it every time. Now I've read that parents should abolish words like maybe, could, might, and possibly from their vocabulary. I'm sorry, but I don't agree. There have been times that my initial response to a request from a child would have been no, but an unexpected change allowed a yes. I'd rather throw out a "maybe" or a "possibly" to allow room for hope. I don't pretend to know exactly what my day holds. So I leave openings for possibilities. I won't lie; there are times that those words have been used to buy time. I don't have all the answers. Sometimes I have to research. I've messed up before and promised something I couldn't possibly deliver. Situations arise that we have absolutely no control over.

Here's an example of when saying "maybe" is appropriate.

One day, despite a bad feeling, I decided to treat the kids to cake at our favorite local cake shop. We were all excited until I found out that they only took cash. I don't carry cash. I gave it up years ago because little school kids were nickel-and-diming me out of my check! Anyway, back to the story. We're at the counter, and I'm fumbling around trying to find the money. I didn't have enough for the kids to get their own favorite piece, and I felt so bad. The mistake wasn't that I had said yes and had to renege, but that I didn't go with my gut and say maybe. So there are times that telling your kids maybe is ok.

One thing, though. Don't use "maybe" when you <u>know</u> it's a "no". That's just stringing someone's feelings along. Be honest. If you know 100% that it's a "no", say it. If you're not sure and it's a "maybe", say it. If it's a "yes", say it. This will pay off in teenage years when you ask your child a question and need a solid answer from them. Think about your life and the things that have occurred. It hasn't always been a clear yes or no initially. So allow your kids to understand that things aren't always cut and dry. There are "if-then" situations (if we leave early enough, then we'll have time) as well as "yes or no" situations (yes, we are going, no we are not).

Compassion

Consider your kid's feelings at their current stage of life before you dish out a consequence. A toddler crying because you took a toy away is not the same as a six-year-old or a teen. Or is it? How would you feel if someone took your cell phone away for a week? I'm not saying this shouldn't be a course of action. I'm just saying to be sure the consequence matches the severity of the infraction. You may not want to keep their cell for a week for missing curfew by 5 minutes. Or maybe you do, just to make a point. However, you don't want it to backfire. Kids are crafty. Not wise (that should be our area of expertise), but crafty. They'll figure out a way to get what they want if given enough time.

For example, I remember wanting to wear miniskirts as a teenager. It was out of the question. I remember my dad seeing me in it and asking, "Whatcha' sellin'?" I said, "Girl Scouts is over. Cookie season is done." I was confused, and the point he was trying to make completely went over my head. He asked again, "Soooo, whatcha' sellin'?" I said, "I'm not selling anything." He said, "You're sure dressed like you are."

Man, did the light bulb go on! I thought I was just trying to look cute like the other girls. I hadn't realized I was trying to look like what my grandmother called a "fast tailed" or "hot in the behind" girl. At that point, I understood what I was doing and why it was wrong. Did it stop me? No. I just complained to my girlfriends, who advised me to sneak out the outfit in my bookbag and change once I got to school. So just know that kids will try to get around or out of what you tell them to do. Oh yeah, I did get busted eventually. I had a teacher ask me if my parents knew I wore *that* to school (gotta love those good, old school teachers!) I told her yes. She said if she saw me in it again, she'd call my parents. Well, she didn't have to do a thing. I forgot to change back into my regular clothes before leaving school that day, and I got grounded.

Committed

The "committed" I'm referring to is dedication, not the one that requires medication. Parenting is not for the faint of heart! Our goal is to train up our kids so that they'll be responsible adults and good citizens. To do that, you'll have to discipline, love, and defend all at the same time.

Discipline is laying down the rules and regulations for any and all situations. Not punishment. Discipline is a clear cut set of cause and effect scenarios that'll inspire your child to make the right decision. It puts the ball in their court before it's technically in yours. Discipline is also a means to remove all emotion from a consequence. It's a way of saying, "You did it, so now you have to deal with the consequences". No ifs, ands, or buts.

I remember watching a commercial about a family whose family calendar also included disciplinary actions. Once it was written down, there was no changing it. It worked! Since it was written down, there were no issues with trying to remember when the consequence starts or ends, what the consequence was or who it was for. It's in black and white for all to see. When I was growing up, the consequences were so outrageous that it made breaking the rules out of the question. I remember that if I brought home grades below a C, I was grounded until the end of the next grading period- *nine weeks*. That made me work hard every day because who in the world wants to be grounded nine weeks?! This may sound extreme (maybe it was), but the proof was in the pudding. The bar my parents set then is the reason for my success today. I was not that motivated to succeed without that expectation in place. However, the right motivation can make all the difference!

Being a parent means loving hard. You have to see past your child's faults and their true intentions and love who they are. You have to see past what would be easy, fun, or popular (for them and for you) and sometimes give tough love. It means seeing past the quick, easy fix, and going with long term solutions. Case in point, there are kids famous for their ridiculous behavior. Kids who make habits of bad behavior end up (in the best case) becoming jerks. Some kids aren't so lucky. It can have morbid consequences if they encounter the wrong situation. We all know the saying, "it's all fun and games until someone gets hurt". It's true! So as parents, we have to nip it in the bud and not only find the right path for them but help them stay on it. Sometimes it's not even in that order!

It also means taking time to see who you're working with. Everyone is different. You hear stories all the time about kids raised in the same house, same parents, same rules, and then one is a valedictorian while the other was a dropout.

Don't beat yourself up if you have different means of

correction for different kids. My two sons are at different ages and have different likes and dislikes. Taking a game system away from the younger means he's gonna dive into his building sets, books, and other toys. He won't shed a single tear but will make the best of a bad situation. He's almost ungroundable! That's not a real word, by the way.

Once, we grounded the child by taking his toys away (I mean ALL of his toys), and the boy played with a toothpick and a ball of fluff!! I won't have to worry about that one. Now, my oldest? He's a whole different story. Taking the game system from my oldest means I have to deal with the dragging, pouting, and mumbling. Granted, I could chalk that up to him being a preteen. However, he has his own way of coping. He's a thinker and an opportunist. If his toys are gone, he'll just go play with someone else's. So what do we do? Ground the whole pre-adult population in the house? No, that doesn't work either. More about that later.

Another way to express commitment is through communication. Take time to hear and especially listen. They're not the same thing. It's like throwing a tennis ball against a wall or a bowling ball into the mud. One bounces off, and the other sinks in. I do allow the kids to express their feelings-within reason and within certain parameters. You can tell me what's on your mind, but you can't yell at an adult, suck your teeth, or roll your eyes. Sorry, being raised by traditional old school parents will only let me go so far. However, the new school in me wants to know what's on your mind so I can see your perspective. I want to be sure I have all the facts and then help you understand how to correctly navigate the situation.

One of my goals as a parent is to teach my kids how to think (not what to think-that's two different things) and to ultimately think on their own and be independent. It sounds glamorous to be this fountain of wisdom and knowledge, but after a list of rapid-fire questions, it can get old. If you don't teach your kids to think on their own, they'll be calling you nonstop about nothing. I know. I've seen it.

I had friends who, God bless them, couldn't go out for an hour without their phone ringing off the hook. For what? "Mommy, where's the peanut butter? When are you coming back? What are you doing? Can I get some snacks from the cabinet?" Mind you, those calls weren't from a little kid. We're talking pre-teen. And the kicker is, Dad <u>was at home</u>!!! These are also not moms who don't spend time with their kids. On the contrary, these were moms who spent a lot of time with their kids. So I'm sure there's a parent out there wondering, when did the unnecessary phone calls stop? I'll tell you. They stopped when they put their foot down and set parameters!

Here's an example of parameters: "Sally, if you have questions, go ask someone who is in the house. If you want to talk to Mommy, you can call Mommy once an hour. No more. I will be home by such-and-such. I love you! Bye." So the child got clear instructions, still knew that Mommy was available, and loved them, but Mommy could get some much needed time out of the house to defrag. Moms need to defragment (aka exhale and reset their minds and emotions), so they can be effective. Same for Dads, but men seem to be able to zone out, tune out, check out, and veg out with no bones about it. You know, be present without being present. Moms seem to need to get away physically and get away from the noise altogether.

Ironically, stepping away briefly (whether physically or mentally) is one of the best ways to stay committed to our kids. It gives us time to back up and take a good look at what we're dealing with while giving us time to come up with a solid plan of action. It helps us stay committed to the path we're on. It takes commitment to lay down the law of your house and stick to it. If you don't, you'll find that your kids will run all over you, or worse.

Champions

Parents should be champions. We must be masters of offense and defense at all times. Being the watchman in front and the defenders in back. I'm reminded of a prophet in the Bible, Nehemiah. In Nehemiah Chapter 4:15-18 it reads (The Message Bible)

15-18 Our enemies learned that we knew all about their plan and that God had frustrated it. And we went back to the wall and went to work. From then on, half of my young men worked while the other half stood guard with lances, shields, bows, and mail armor. Military officers served as backup for everyone in Judah, who was at work rebuilding the wall. The common laborers held a tool in one hand and a spear in the other. Each of the builders had a sword strapped to his side as he worked. I kept the trumpeter at my side to sound the alert.

This is a picture you should remember. This is what you're doing. You're building up your kids while the world tries to tear them down through fear tactics, unruly behavior, lack of self-control, etc. Too vague? I'll be more specific. Lies, deceit, media hype, poor role models on TV, drinking, drugs (prescribed or not), premarital sex, bullying, kidnapping, and well, you get the idea. It's a tough deal, but this is what we've signed up for. However, I've written this book in hopes that it'll help someone.

2 KEEP IT TOGETHER-ORGANIZATION

One of the best things I've seen to make parenting easier is bookkeeping. I know it sounds a little off, but hear me out. If you write things down, there's less for you to remember. One thing my husband used to say that really rattled my cage was, "Baby, those kids have completely destroyed your mind! With every kid we've had, you've lost more of your mind." Shoot, what did he expect? I went from remembering my stuff (when I was single) to remembering *our* stuff (when we got married), to remembering *five people's stuff*!!! <u>THAT'S</u> why moms are crazy and easily provoked. We have too much going on to deal with foolishness. So no, people, it's not all pixie dust and rainbows over here. We've got business to take care of!

Ok, let me put my soapbox back in its golden case. You can put your banners and confetti away. But I know you can relate. So here are some cool ideas to keep everything straight and not lose your mind.

Family Calendar

Whether paper, dry erase, or electronic, having a family calendar can alleviate a lot of confusion and stress. Logging tasks, homework, bills, grocery lists, meals, and date nights keeps them in a place where the entire family has access. It's hard to follow an unwritten plan.

And the LORD answered me, and said, Write the vision, and make it plain upon tables, that he may run that readeth it. Habakkuk 2:2 King James Version (KJV)

So when you and your family come up with a plan, keep it simple, straightforward, and easy to follow! You can use different colors for different types of events (work, church, school, community, sports) or for the person they correspond to (Mom, Dad, kids, pets). This will reveal the entire family schedule but still keep it organized according to each person.

My husband and I decided from here on out we'll have the same brand of phone so that we can sync everything. It's also handy if I have to run out and my battery is low. He'll switch with me and let his charge or vice versa. If your kids have phones, you can sync with them, too. Keep all calendars in sync, and it'll be smoother sailing when unexpected events pop up.

Arts and Crafts Area

Having an area mandated for all things artsy and craftsy keeps the kids focused and allows all potential messes to be contained in a specific area. Be sure it's an area that is "oops" resistant (no carpet, dent resistant, glue, and glitter tolerant). It may help for it to be near a window. Sometimes fumes from spray glue, paint, and cleaners will need to be ventilated. If you've dedicated an entire room or part of a room, maybe hang or frame their art there for display. That way, there's less to store.

We let the kids hang their art in their room, so we don't have so much to store. My daughter is currently in the "making things for Mommy" (constantly) stage, so I got a notebook filled with clear sleeves and started collecting her artwork. This will be neatly stored in the mementos area of the hall closet or the family room bookshelf for browsing. The boys are a bit different. The middle one is eight, and the oldest is 12, so they're into building 3D things. I can just take pics with my phone and put them on my flash drive.

Files for Each Child

If you have multiples, keeping a set of files for each child will become more important as they grow older. Once those school records, health records, awards, and other documents start to pile up, you want to be able to find them easily. Consider separating them by file folder color or design or file documents according to age. There are also hanging wall folders for families with multiple children. Label each folder and keep their papers on the side of the fridge, on the inside of the pantry door, or on the pantry wall. Anywhere that is accessible but out of the way will work best.

Command Station

What's a command station, you ask? It's the central nervous system of your house. It's where each and every member can get and give information and resources for your entire family. Here are some great items to have in your command station.

Family calendar

Chore charts

Grocery lists

Clips for coupons (form making returns or for doing your budget)

Suction cup containers full of whiteboard markers

Erasers

Magnets

Drawers for papers

Standing files

Pouches

Crates

Shelves

Cabinets

Carts

Notebooks

All of these things are great ways to organize. Don't forget hooks for keys (great for driving or latchkey teens). You can also include pins or pegs for holding items in place or as cute hangers. You can immediately see whose keys are missing and see who is in or out of the house.

Chore Chart

My family has a chore can (I mentioned it earlier in the book), but a chore chart works better for some. I've seen some cool ideas for custom ones lately. The most recent one was a DIY version where cookie sheets were spray-painted, and magnets with different chores were placed in one of two areas on the sheet, "to do" and "done". How cool is that?!

Other versions were laminated checklists for each family member, each day or each room. I saw one that had a numberless calendar placed inside a clear sleeve, and they used dry erase markers to write the numbers and events. You can use different colors for different types of events (work, church, school, community, sports) or for the person they correspond to (Mom, Dad, kids, pets).

Grocery List

To make my grocery shopping easier, I put a dry erase board on the side of the fridge. I used to take a picture of the list. I found that to be a pain because I couldn't check off what I'd put in the grocery cart. Now, I use an app called ColorNote to make my lists.

Before that, I used a laminated grocery list that was like a checklist, but it was not respected or utilized by the kids. As soon as they were able to read and/or write, I had them begin to add items to the list. It helped them practice their reading and writing skills. The biggest thing was to train them to write items down when we got low or if they used the last of something. This lessened my stress because I didn't have to do the kitchen run-down (aka the "what do we need" game). Now they do it without being asked and even leave me love notes (or hate mail when I take too long to buy popcorn for family movie time). It cut down the prep time for meals, and when I was about to go to the grocery store, I could take a picture of the list with my phone or key it into my ColorNote app. This app allows you to write text or checklists and color code them. You can email them or share them (great for sending your husband honey-do lists on the fly), and you can even put an alarm or reminder on it! My husband even has a grocery cart app that allows you to use a slider to add the price of items as you put them in the cart, so there are no surprises at checkout when the total rings up. So cool!

Family Photos

We used to take pictures and print them. No more! The task was just too much. We take a lot of pictures. So we keep them on a flash drive. Now we can share them whenever we want, and with basic software which was already pre-installed on our computer, we can create videos and all kinds of fun media! It cut down the clutter, reduced our need for expensive printer ink and for photo paper. Not to mention the time it takes to get them prepped to print (you've almost always have to crop something). So if grandparents want pics, just email them (assuming they have a computer to view them). I remembered when I was ahead of my parents in the technology realm. One big motivator for them to get up to date on technology was them getting pictures of the kids on their phone. They wanted to print them, so they went out and got a printer just for pictures. They've been techies ever since! Which is great for us because we can share a ton of family photos with little to no expense.

Hidden Storage

When you have kids, you have pirates. Cute though they may be, they're dangerous (to themselves and others). I've learned that I must hide things from them so they won't get hurt and also so I can use my own stuff! I have innocent-looking cans and boxes in my office that, to the untrained eye, appear to be uninteresting. I learned this golden nugget one day when I ate all my "Mommy-only" hazelnut chocolate artisan rolled wafers. The can is so pretty that I decided to keep it. It also reminds me of Paris…bonus! Anyway, the little people in my house had been stealing my pens, Sharpies, and other items. So I stashed them in there! Ok, I confess, this is not my own unique idea. As a child, my mom stored all of the empty Christmas boxes, bag, and bows in one huge box that was wrapped like a present. Daddy and I fell for that one for at least two years! Now I use this method to keep our adult stuff out of little hands.

Food, Snack, and Lunch Storage

I love Pinterest! You can go on there (even without an account) and find all manner of things that will help you through life. *Side note: go to pinterest.com and in the search bar type "hack" and push enter. You'll be on there for God knows how long finding things to make life simpler. You're welcome!

Anyway, back to the topic at hand. You can use all kinds of things to make packing lunches easier. Whether for school, camping, picnics in the yard, it can be a task to find everything you need, prep, and make the meal and clean up quickly. One idea I saw used two 3-drawer carts to house all of the paper bags, baggies, straws, napkins, dry snacks, etc. This was known as the lunch station. So cool! Since everything is in one place and readily visible, you have everything in one place, see what's running low and what you're out of.

Color Code Your Kids!

We have a problem in our house. We do way too much laundry. One way to figure out the culprit is to color-code your kids. Assign a color to them (or let them pick), so you can see whose color gets the most rotation in the laundry. Instead of colors, you can also use monograms or themes (cartoon characters, favorite team, etc.) Now you know who to isolate to talk to. I don't know about you, but I hate it when my boss pulls everyone off the work we're doing to talk (fuss) about something one person did instead of pulling that individual to the side!

Another important thing to do is teach about "laundry longevity". We had to teach our kids how long to keep their towels, sheets, washcloths, etc. before they should get a new one. Otherwise, one would keep it a day while another would keep it until it walked off on its own. Color coding also ends the "Bubba took my washcloth" arguments. Not to mention the "Who left their washcloth in the tub again?" inquisitions.

I know part of it is the fact that their laundry hampers were too small. Once they passed age 5, they needed bigger hampers. The other issue was school. When school is in, they have school clothes, play clothes and nightclothes. Especially when they were in private school. This makes laundry a beast! Every time you turned around, someone didn't have enough clean socks, collared shirts, skirts, whatever. More clothes seemed to mean more laundry and more problems. So we ended up getting larger hampers, and that cut down on how often laundry was done. We also got more selective with what was washed and when. Jeans don't need to be washed every week. Now we're a bit looser with their clothes since they're in public school. Their school clothes are (in a lot of cases) their play clothes.

However, we found out one of their tricks. When they washed their laundry (yes, we make *them* wash their own little funky clothes-more about that later), they'd take it upstairs, but not put it away. Then, they'd put dirty clothes on top of clean in the hamper and three days later had clothes climbing up the wall again! It took us a while to figure it out, but our solution was to make them hang up everything before they left our sight. Sometimes we make an event out of it and hang up clothes during family time. We sort the clean clothes together, send them up one at a time with their clothes and then sit and hang them up together. *TIP: If their hamper is getting too full too soon, do what we did. Make them smell their own clothes and separate dirty from clean before washing.

3 HERDING THE SHEEP

(PUTTING A SYSTEM IN PLACE)

Every institution needs a system in place in order to be successful. Families are the same way. Every family needs a system to remain healthy and happy. The system should be customized to the individual family, and because people grow and change, the system is subject to change at any moment for optimal performance. Here are some ideas to help you keep your system running!

Time Out or Time In

Some parents use the time out method. Traditionally this is done by designating a predetermined amount of time in a specific place where a child sits and thinks about what they did and how to avoid the mistake the next time the opportunity arises. There are variations about times set by the offense or by the age of the child.

Time-outs don't work for every child, so you may want to try a "time-in." This is done by having your child complete a task that has a clearly defined beginning and end. Tasks could be assembling a small puzzle, stacking blocks into a particular pattern, or tracing ABCs. A time-in is meant to diffuse the anger and put focus on a likable task that is viewed as positive.

Use a Timer

Timers are great for setting clearly defined boundaries. For example, you can say, "I want you to clean your room, fold the laundry, sweep the floor, etc. in 10 minutes. The timer is on. If you haven't finished by then, your correction is…." This method helps them be more focused and self-motivated. It also leaves little or no wiggle room on the matter. I use the microwave timer button or the timer app on my phone. They are both crazy loud, so there's no excuse about not hearing it. If you decide to include correction or consequence, consider having them repeat the exercise until they can get it done in the allotted time(no matter how redundant). It will make them more motivated and detail-oriented. Not to mention that they'll be great problem solvers. They'll have to look at why they're doing the job (to avoid doing it again) and how they're doing it (can this get done faster? Better?). Great training for the real world!

Create a Consequence Can

Make a can and fill it with cut-up index cards with different corrections or consequences on them. Make them choose. Whatever they get is not your fault or your choice (not directly, anyway). Some options to consider are no electronic devices for a night, writing a letter on why what they did was wrong, going to bed early, etc. Depending on the severity of the infraction, you can tell them to get two (I hope it's not that bad). In our house, there are a few "get off easy" cards where they only have to kiss or hug a parent, do a sibling's (or parent's) chore, make a greeting card to the person they harmed saying they're sorry, etc. Some can be blank to reflect on how we can receive mercy when we deserve a punishment. Another option to throw in blank cards as an opportunity to talk about how God gives us mercy even when we deserve punishment.

Ridiculous Tasks

Once, my kids wouldn't stop fussing and touching each other as we were driving to our destination. Their "punishment" was to make fish lips and kiss their knee. You should've seen them trying to figure that one out! They got to giggling so hard that they stopped fighting and started encouraging each other! Another crazy idea is to have them stand nose to nose (if you have multiple kids) for a ten count. I've tried some other interesting ideas like the "get along t-shirt" (didn't like it-they actually fought <u>more</u>), and the most effective: "doody duty". How does it work? It requires a pooper scooper, shovel, or doody bags, and one misbehaving child. To be clear, this is reserved for the behaviors I dislike the most: kids who don't listen or act like they've got amnesia. You know how it is. You tell them to do something, and they ignore you or conveniently forget to do it. "Doody duty" ended that real quick! They usually had to serve 5 minutes. However, if the same offense was repeated the same day, the time was increased. Oh, don't think you have to have a pet to use this method. Someone somewhere has a pet who's doing their business. You can even find a lonely person with a pet or a pet-friendly community for the aging who'd love to see more kids around. Now I don't do some real old school methods like cutting grass with nail clippers or scissors for a short time (even though I see why it'd work wonders). In this day and age, anything to make our kids pay more attention to what they're doing and why is a good thing.

Come Off the Hinges

Not you, the door! If you're always catching your kid in their room in some random act of foolishness, take the door off the hinges. This also works great for teenagers who are on the "privacy" soapbox. Don't get me wrong, I believe in teenagers having their privacy, personal space and a safe place to escape from the issues of life. However, if the reason is to shut you out, disrespect you (or the household), or so they can do things that are contrary to the moral theme of your household, take the door off the hinges until they can prove they can be trusted and respectful.

Lights Out (Modified)

When I was a kid, I got sent to bed at a moment's notice. Usually, it was because I was exhibiting traits of a kid who needed a nap. As an alternative, you can move the bedtime up as it relates to their behavior that day. For each bad choice, move the time up by five, ten, fifteen, or more minutes. Alternately, extend their time for good behavior, good choices, and good accomplishments. That way, they can see the consequences of their actions and how they can affect the rest of their day.

Driver's Dilemmas

I remember a kid from my high school who broke a house rule and had to wait another year to get their license. We all cried for them!! Talk about hitting a teenage kid where it hurts! Restricting use of a license, permit, or vehicle is big!

I saw a great trick on a commercial advertising a car with a rear camera (the kind that allows you to see behind you when you back up). If you don't want your kids to sneak and take the car, consider this. The parent wrote the car mileage in sidewalk chalk on the driveway along with the message, "NICE TRY-DAD". When the kid was leaving the driveway, he saw the message in the camera and promptly put the car back.

There are other methods, like the car you use to lock the steering wheel, take the spare car keys when you leave, leave the keys with a friend or neighbor, or use tracking devices or apps to bust them. Confronting a situation after the occurrence is also a great way to deal with the problem. *If you've noticed the car being moved and you've confiscated the key, they may have wised up and made an extra copy. No worries. Remember the bar that locks the steering wheel? Yeah, they still make those.

Self-Control May Be the Issue

Self-Control is highly underrated. Self-control is the fuel which causes us to get anything and everything done on a daily basis. Think about your day. Do you want to get up early? No. Why do you do it? Self-control. What needs to be done outweighs the feelings about how it must get done. So, as much as we don't enjoy doing some things, self-control is the mechanism we use to make progress.

Here are some things that require self-control that we may not think about:

Starting tasks in a timely manner

Having a good attitude in a bad situation

Responding to a request immediately (if possible)

Keeping a schedule (morning routine, daily schedule, etc.)

Ok, so maybe you do see how these things take self-control. Well, did you consider that the reason challenges arise with children is because they haven't learned it? Ask yourself:

When corrected, does my child have a good attitude?

When in a team environment, does my child abide by the rules? Do they do their best? Do they even try to have fun?

Does my child follow schedules (bedtime, chores), are they unselfish or do they take turns without being told?

Or...

Do they have a bad or violent response when corrected?

Do they break the rules, do subpar work, or are they often competitive?

Do they neglect or overlook schedules, only think about themselves, or interrupt others?

Finally, where do they see these behaviors modeled?

Is there honest, constructive discussion about why these traits are positive or negative?

4 COMMUNICATION AND DISAGREEMENTS

The 1-2-3-4-5 system

Think about this method I came up with (it may work for you, it may not). There are five different ways you can communicate with your teen (or any age group, really). I call them the five levels. Level 1 is DO NOTHING. Level 2 is LISTEN. Level 3 is GIVE ADVICE. Level 4 is HELP. Level 5 is HANDLE.

How do these levels work? I'll explain. Level 1 is do nothing. Yes, I said it. Do <u>absolutely nothing</u>. Let them work it through on their own, but you still be aware of the situation. Ever walk past your child while they're in conversation about a problem? Some require you to do nothing but be aware of the situation. They can figure out some things for themselves.

Level 2 is listening. If your daughter comes home upset and wants to talk, listen. Just listen. Then ask if she just wanted to vent or if she needs your help in any way. Usually, kids will ask for help if they need it (you may or may not actually hear the question within all of the drama and/or crying). If you don't hear them ask for help, ask if they <u>want</u> you to help and <u>ask HOW</u>. Stick to what they ask (unless it'll really, really hurt them if you don't) so that you'll build trust. If they need more help than they're asking for, <u>gently</u> insert a suggestion.

Level 3 is advice. Sometimes they know what the problem is but may not know what the solution is. Sometimes they know what the solution is, but need to know where to start. Be sure to give them what they need, but not too much more. Otherwise, you may see the glazed over look (they've mentally checked out), the blank stare (you've overwhelmed them with too much information), or you may hear, "Mooooom, I'm not stupid." or "Daaad, geez! I'm not a baby."

Level 4 is help. Wouldn't it be great if they came out and asked for it? Well, when they do, make sure you're ready. However, like any good manager, find out what they really want and exactly how to deliver. Also, do it in such a way so that nothing is lost, and no injury occurs (if possible).

Level 5 is handle it. Some things require your intervention (and them getting out of the picture). Whether it's speaking to a teacher on your child's behalf or calling the cops, there are situations that they should just stay out of.

All this advice is great, but the biggest thing (as I said before) is knowing how and when to do it. That's where you come in. You must know your child and know yourself. You may not be the person to do each one of these steps. Sometimes as a mom, I can't handle some situations. Once my oldest had to go to the ER and had to have hand surgery. I couldn't do it. That's Dad territory 1000%. Take the middle child to the ER three times in one week at 2 a.m. because he was wheezing and wouldn't stop? I could do that with no problem. Grandparents may need to step in, aunts and uncles may be the go-to for some scenarios. Don't count out friends, community members, church members, mentors, teachers, etc. It takes a village!

Arguing Siblings

Man, I could fill a library with the ridiculous arguments my kids have had! It honestly grates my nerves. The worst part is, it's the same stupid arguments. To top it off, my husband says it's normal. He has a younger brother, and I'm an only child, so he's used to it. I guess being an only child is the main reason why I like peace among family members. So there's where those perspectives come from. The funny thing is, I'd prefer them to talk it out, and he lets them fuss it out. Thank God our kids aren't violent (we have white carpet). I don't know if letting them fuss it out is always a good course of action. Anyway, on to some solutions…

Cool Down Time

Send each contender to their corner (their room or another room). You may have them write down why they're upset or let them scream how they feel into their pillow (pillow talk). Keep in mind that some children take longer to cool down than others, and some offenses are greater than others. Be patient, be practical, and be compassionate. Putting yourself in their shoes at *their age* can change the way you address the situation.

Talk It Out

Have a family meeting. Have both sides present their case. Ask pertinent questions that aren't easy to wiggle out of. Make a decision and issue a decree for how to fix the situation and mend the relationship. If they're of age, allow the kids to work it out themselves, but still be present (if necessary), so you are aware of the climate of your house. I can't tell you how many parents have said they heard their teen but didn't listen. An argument that seems as small as "stay out of my room" was actually "I'm viewing inappropriate material and don't need you getting me busted". Keep your eyes peeled and your ears open!

Act It Out

Use socks, stuffed animals, or puppets to show the kids how they're behaving. If nothing else, it'll get everyone laughing and break the tension. Then talk about what the real problem is and how it can be solved. Don't dismiss this for older children. You'd be surprised what you'll learn by introducing a nontraditional method to work out a problem. I've seen kids giggling through an impromptu sketch when they were about to kill one another seconds earlier.

Why Are They Right?

Instead of expressing why *you* are right, do a role reversal between kids and have them explain why their sibling is right or why they may feel the way they do. Be ready to laugh or cry. You never know what'll come out of their mouths. Also, set some ground rules, so they aren't even *more* offensive or destructive to the relationship (or your mental state). Try to have fun with it!

Co-Chore

Have them complete a chore (clean out the garage, trim the shrubs, de-poop the back yard) that gives them time alone to talk it out. Sometimes, especially with boys, the physicality of a job opens them up to discuss their feelings. I don't know why (remember that "I'm not a psychologist" disclaimer?), but it works. It works with catch, basketball, tennis or any other sport where you're facing each other. It can be something they like to do or something they hate. For whatever reason, I've seen it work a million times. Ask anyone who's had to wash dishes, fold laundry, or rake the yard with a sibling. At some point, you'll chill out and/or talk it out.

Stop Talking

If you keep telling your child the same thing over and over, stop! Change the expectation. Just start dishing out the consequence. When you tell them their consequence, and they ask why they're in trouble, tell them. Let them know the consequence will continue and/or escalate until they decide to make the right choice. For example, when my kids are messing up, I'll send them to the chore can without saying why. Then if they ask why, then I tell them. In some cases, they don't ask why, because they already knew they were wrong.

Listen. No Really, LISTEN.

Teens believe that you have no clue and never will. If you're not a transparent parent, now is the time to start being one. I had a discussion with my oldest the other day about prayer. He thought that I didn't talk to God at all. I almost fainted! He thought Daddy was the big prayer of the household. I couldn't help it. I had to tell him. "You think only DADDY prays? Who do you think is always praying that Daddy <u>will</u> pray?!" Crazy kid. Anyway, I had to be open. I had to tell him, that's why Mommy is up at 5 am. That's why I am toting around that crazy looking notebook and going off to Bible study and meetings at church. It is <u>NOT</u> to be seen! I'd rather be home in the jammies with snacks (sad, but true). Then he got the look on his face, "Oh, you *ARE* human!" Yeah, kiddo. Mommy is human. Does your kid know that you messed up as a kid? As an adult? A few minutes ago?? When you listen and observe them, they're more likely to do the same to you.

I had to tell my kids about a mistake I made about a year ago when I didn't tell my boss something really, really important because I was trying to shield a mentee from the fallout of her poor choice. In the heat of the moment, I thought I was protecting her. After thinking it through, I was going to get three people in trouble as opposed to letting her take the heat for her error. So I had to 'fess up, let him know about the situation and apologize for my poor choice as well. When I did, the situation turned out to be microscopic. But getting up the courage to come clean was really hard. I realized I was acting just like a kid. I'd chosen to hide something while trying to fix it and hoping for the best until it was resolved. My kids were floored! From then on, we didn't have that gap of "my parents don't understand what I'm going through". Be transparent with your kids so they'll do the same with you. The last thing a family needs is secrets.

Don't Make It Personal

Don't bring up their personal shortcomings or imperfections, because they will do the same to you. That gets you nowhere fast. Attacking a child is no way to parent. Calling your children names destroys the delicate fabric of your relationship in a way that is very difficult to repair.

Another bad idea is talking about their other parent in the midst of a heated discussion. Phrases like "You act just like your Daddy" or "I hate it when you say that, you sound just like your Mother" are devastating to children. It creates confusion. How are they not supposed to look, act, and sound like their other parent? Children naturally love their parents, and our job is to continue the love flow, not cut it off, no matter what our feelings are about the other person.

Don't Talk Through Your Children

Also, don't say things to your child that you really want to say to their other parent. That is "speaking through" your child. This leaves your child in the position of hearing messages that they shouldn't always be privy to. Sometimes they may think they're the reason for the conversation. It creates a burden to them that they should not have to bear. They are not living, breathing walkie talkies, so deliver your own message. It'll lead to them taking sides against a parent.

Keep in mind that having them take information back and forth puts them in a conversation that is not their own. That plants seeds for "he said, she said". I've seen parents discuss things in front of their children that are inappropriate. I'm not talking about intimate things necessarily, but gossip. Do you want your child to gossip? No? Then don't bring up other people's business in front of them. Turn off the speakerphone, go to a secluded area to have private conversations, and don't give them the play by play about who did what. It won't hurt them to avoid those reality TV garbage fests, either.

Don't Generalize

In the heat of a disagreement, resist the urge to use phrases like "you always", "you never", "every time you…", etc. Generalizations, insults, and rants are just cues for kids to shut their ears off and shut down. Not to mention shut you out! Be calm and address the actual issue. Generalizations are also exaggerations. Being clear and specific in conversations is very important.

Consider this. When a teen says something is "not a big deal", do you want to <u>know</u> that it's not? Or do you want them to have a skewed understanding of the size of a matter? If you want them to have an accurate perspective, start them off with a good measuring stick. Otherwise, they'll say wrecking your car "isn't such a big deal". Getting a girl pregnant won't be "such a big deal". Doing drugs won't be "a big deal". Looking at inappropriate material on the computer won't be "a big deal". Is that how we want them to think? Then don't generalize. If you don't generalize with small matters and it won't carry over to larger ones as they mature and grow into adults.

Don't Jump to Conclusions

Be sure to find what the issue really is before trying to address it. Here's an example. My kids were driving my husband and I nuts because they didn't want to do their chores. Shoot, who does? Anyway, while discussing doing dishes, I told my husband a childhood story about doing them when I was young. We figured out at that instant why

I don't like doing dishes and avoid hand washing dishes like the plague. It gave my husband insight into his wife he'd never known before. It gave me insight about me that I'd never realized! So before jumping to conclusions like, "the child is just lazy", find out the real problem. Check the time of day you ask them to do something. Giving them chores immediately after school, right before bed or right before homework may not be good for them? How do you feel about coming in from work and immediately cleaning the house? Wouldn't you like at least 10-30 minutes to rest before getting started? Sit down and calmly discuss their schedule. Let them give you ideas. Kids aren't just here to learn from us. We need to take the opportunities we have to learn from them. If you find that the reason is laziness, at least you have the peace of knowing you heard them out!

Don't Pick Fights

I don't know why, but some parents love to antagonize their kids. They feel that's their right as a parent. That's not good parenting. That's bullying. This one is a biggie with fathers and sons. I don't know why, but some fathers seem to get a thrill out of tormenting their children by pushing their buttons. What are you really trying to accomplish? If you want your child to do their best, start by comforting them, then encouraging them.

Give compliments: great job, that was really nice, I saw what you did there, way to go! Tthen try to make correction in an encouraging way: maybe next time try this, you may get even better results if you do _____, don't give up kiddo you'll get it, Rome wasn't built in a day, how about trying this?

They'll see that you actually care about them, not the issue. Kids want to know that what they do is special in your eyes. When you attack or belittle them, they will put up walls, lash out or sometimes crumble. Don't do that to them. The world does it enough to us. We don't need to do it to our kids.

I remember when I was a teen, my dad used to get on my last ever-loving nerve by doing crazy stuff to me! Once I got in trouble with my mom for black handprints on the walls in the hallway. I had to prove to her it wasn't me because Daddy told her *I* did it! Thank God I had small hands. I had to play Perry Mason and show her the print was too big to be mine. Boy, did he get in trouble with my mom! But, what goes around comes around. Finally, think about this: you're harassing the person who'll pick your old folks home! That's just not wise. So be mindful of the consequences of your actions and your words.

Stop Trying to Figure out Who Wins

Having back and forths with your kids is never progressive unless it leads to the root of an issue. Parents often want to "win" no matter what. Pick your battles carefully. Your child needs to learn that winning isn't the most important thing. Staying in the "sweet spot" is. You know that lovely place where everyone is happy, getting along and civil? Sometimes peace is more important than a prize. I don't mean taking a dive on every issue, but consider this: will it matter tomorrow? In a year? In 5-10 years? If so, put your foot down or come to some reasonable agreement. If not, let it go! Instead of trying to show how right you are (or wrong they are), take a step back and see if the issue you're fighting about is worth the harm to the relationship.

Ask Questions

Do you try to find out who your child is? What they like, how they think, how they learn, what their future plans are, and why? Or are you an auto-pilot parent, serving as a parent like it's a prison sentence? The joking side of this book is that we want to survive until it's time for our kids to be on their own. But the serious side of this book is that as much as we're trying to get to that point, we want to do it successfully, and everyone come out on top.

A family is a team working toward the same goal! So make every effort to know your kids. Favorite food, color, pastime, season, animal, everything! How can you live with someone 18 years and not know them? Don't just boss them around and expect them to fall in line. That's a BOSS, not a parent.

The Talking Stick

I read an article on using the talking stick and thought it was such a cool and effective idea! The talking stick has roots in the Native American culture and is used by members of the council. The stick is passed from member to member and allows each person to express their opinion without interruption by others. The other purpose is to encourage attentive listening, to respect another person's point of view and to foster acceptance even when you disagree.

Decide what object should be used as a talking stick. It doesn't even have to be a stick. If you have a prized possession such as a grandparent's Bible, a parent's keepsake, or a family photo, it can help everyone focus on the important things: family, togetherness, respect, and love. If you know for a fact that this will take a lot for your family to adjust to (for those who often talk over one another all the time or yell), then come up with creative ways to encourage them to stop. You may have to hug the person you're angry with for 10 seconds. It's longer than it sounds when you want to choke someone! They may lose a turn with the stick if they talk out of turn. You may decide to come up with something else. Figure out what works for your family to help everyone get along and keep the peace!

Walk Down Memory Lane

Do you remember when you had the same arguments with your parents that you're having with your own kids right now? How did you feel as a child? Try to see it through those eyes again (even if your child is wrong) and be a little more compassionate. You may find that the situation isn't as serious as you thought or that there's another way to handle it so that everyone feels like they've been heard. State that you hear them. Say it in their words, then in your own. Explain that you know how it feels. That is not the same as saying it in your own words. Here's a scenario:

Billy: Dad, why is my bedtime so early? I don't have enough time to have fun after school. It's not fair! Why can't I stay up later?

Dad: I hear you, son. You want more time to have fun after school to do what you want to do. I know you want more time to play outside or watch tv or just hang out. I get that. I feel the same way about going to work sometimes. How about we take some time to figure out how we can rearrange your schedule to give you more time to enjoy yourself? After we look at it, you may have more time than you think. But if not, we'll look at changing your bedtime.

If you approach their concerns in a manner which reaches out to them and addresses their needs, they'll be more receptive to open up more, and with time, they'll eventually listen. Note that Dad didn't automatically say yes or no. As parents, we must remember how it felt to get shut down when we asked for something. Walk down memory lane and try a different path. You may find treasure at the end-a better relationship with your child.

Don't Escalate or Retaliate

Kids need to see you handle situations with tact. Instead of yelling, stomping, slamming, or throwing, show them how to behave like an adult. Don't make a small matter worse by taking them to a higher level. Don't go tit for tat, either. Keep a level head when dealing with your kids. Stick to your guns, but at the same time, be sure you don't fall into the emotional trap of reacting in a childlike manner. Remember, _YOU'RE_ the adult!

Do You Have a Safety Zone for Family Concerns?

One of the best ideas my husband had was to create a family forum (family meeting). It allowed any member of the family to call all members to hear their concern. The rules are that everyone must come, everyone must listen, and no one can judge, punish, laugh off, or ignore the situation brought before the family. Usually, we end up coming to a good solution for everyone involved. Ok, we usually end up hearing the person out, coming to a joint decision with consequences if necessary, then acting silly and having family time.

You'd be surprised what kids will call a family meeting for. Things like not enough family time, one of the kids keeps taking stuff from the other, Mommy is gonna ship you off in a small box with a skunk in it if you don't stop leaving things on when you leave the room, Daddy is too stressed out and is acting like a grumpy old fart. You know, normal family stuff. However, there are times when there are serious things like sick friends, bad things that happened at school, or "I'm gonna lose it if" sessions. So try to take time with your family (as much as you can) to make these lines of communication open and available. It teaches kids that everyone (not just them) has a right to speak their mind, be heard without fearing judgment or punishment.

Meet Them Halfway

My grandmother would turn over in her grave if she wasn't already in heaven. Old School Rule # 1 is: The parent is always right (even when they're wrong), and the child will do exactly what the parent says no matter what! So by saying to meet them halfway, I'm negating this rule. As a mom of three, sometimes, I don't care. I couldn't care less about being right. I don't want right or wrong. I want peace. For everyone!

You didn't your bed made in the first five minutes that your feet hit the floor? So what?! Get your little self ready for school and do it when you get home. I'm not sending anyone in there, anyway! You're full and can't eat the rest of your dinner? So what?! Put it in the fridge and you'll eat it when you are hungry again. Didn't finish your homework before bed? So what?! Guess what you're doing before breakfast tomorrow?

There should not be so much strife in our homes that parents are tense, angry, or sick of being parents. Children shouldn't live in constant fear, thinking, "What are they gonna fuss about this time?" Enough! Have peace in your home. If chores are a chore, work something out. I HATE cleaning Saturday morning because it was demanded in my childhood home. So in our home, we do a little every day so we can have more family time on Saturdays. Or just sleep in and walk around in jammies until we are tired of smelling each other. Shoot, we're family!!! We were put together to enjoy each other, not tolerate each other until one moves out or dies. If a subject is causing you to constantly lose your temper, you may need to look at yourself, not the children. You are the grownup, so why is this problem causing you so much turmoil?

Never Compare Your Child to Someone Else Or Something Else

I've seen parents compare one child to the other, and it always ends in disaster. They'll fight between one another, try to outdo one another, and use your affection as a prize to be earned instead of something to be cherished. Don't even compare them to yourself! If you put yourself on a pedestal, you'll just push them away.

I've read parenting advice that says don't tell your teen how you would've been punished for behaving the way they did. If you're saying that to get parenting kudos, don't. It doesn't do any good because of the generation gap. However, sometimes kids need a reality check. They think their world is the only one that exists. There are times they need to understand that the consequences could be worse.

Giving them exposure to the world around them (like letting them watch the news) can be a great eye-opener. Ultimately, accept them as they are and let them know you do by giving them praise for what they accomplish even if it's not up to your personal standards.

Share Your Recent Mistakes and How to Correct Them

While writing this book, I interviewed a close friend of our family. She has three daughters that are all grown up now and have their own families. I asked her to give me one thing that she wished parents knew about parenting. Her advice was this: Be honest with your kids. Don't let them think you were the straightest arrow when you were out doing dirt at their age. Talk to them about the temptations and how you overcame them. Problems come when you put yourself on a pedestal, and your child feels they have to be perfect all the time. I couldn't agree more!

Tell your child how you messed up and how you plan to fix it. Ask their opinion. You'd be surprised what they'll say. I forgot to do something for my husband, and when I shared it with my kids, they gave me information I wasn't aware of. I was going to get him one thing, but after talking with the kids, I realized it wouldn't be the best choice. I still had to apologize to my husband, but at least he got the item he really wanted instead of a less desired runner up!

I saw this idea and thought it was interesting, to say the least! I haven't tried this one, but it might just work. Here it is (paraphrased):

Stop arguing with your teen and type out the situation EXACTLY as it took place without exaggeration and write it as if it was a script for a play. Give everyone involved some time to calm down and then read them the script.

The author said that she usually got an apology when this method was used.

I had to use a similar method with my children when they would make disrespectful faces. You know, eye-rolling and the "whatever" face and all that. I finally realized that my children didn't know that they were making a face! When I showed them the face they were making, they were surprised at themselves. That made it a lot easier for all involved. Nothing is worse than issuing a consequence for a behavior and the recipient not knowing why. That breeds bitterness and contempt toward the parent.

5 KID STUFF

(STUFF KIDS JUST <u>DO</u>-BEHAVIOR MODIFICATION)

Before I get into the "meat" of this section, I'd like to address one thing. As a parent, teacher, and mentor, I've noticed that children often misbehave due to lack of positive attention. I've observed it with my own kids, kids of many friends, students, etc. When children need quality time, they'll find a way to get your attention. Sometimes it's with bad behavior. Before you determine a consequence for your child's actions, spend some time talking with them first. Find out what's really going on. You may still find the need to discipline them for an action, but you may find that they were bored (no one to do something with), angry or confused(no one to express or sort out their feelings with) or having challenges with self-esteem (no one to seek counsel from).

Case in point, there was a little boy I knew that was a tremendous terror. He'd bite, throw things, cuss, have fits of rage and lie. No one wanted to be around him, and his reputation was really bad. The worst thing was, he was only in elementary school! However, it was discovered that all he needed was to spend time alone with his mom. He had a lot of siblings, and he felt overlooked. So how would he get his Mom's attention? Acting out. The remedy? Mommy-son dates! In no time at all, the change was noticed, and it's been smooth sailing from then on (for the most part-he's still a kid)!

Without further ado, behavior modification tips!

The Touchers

Children touch stuff. All the time. Anyplace. In some environments, that's ok. Babies are expected to touch stuff. That's not what I mean. I mean when children *who know better* touch other people's things. I have three children and "Maaaaa! _____ is touching my stuff! Mommy, tell _____ to stop touching my stuff!" was heard at least four to five times a day. Even my husband was complaining about his stuff being touched by the children. Until I'd had enough. I came up with this crazy rule: If you touched someone else's stuff, you had to clean their room. No matter whose stuff or what room. Touch your brother's/sister's stuff, and you have to clean their room. Touch

Mommy's/Daddy's office stuff, and you have to clean that respective office. I am glad to report that it worked! I haven't found my notepads in my daughter's room or my husband's pens in my son's rooms or anything. If the children have touched each other's stuff, I haven't heard about it. So they either stopped, or they have an underground agreement to not snitch. Either way, it works for me!

Address it the First Time

When your child does something, you don't want them to continue (such as tantrums, backtalk, or breaking curfew), address it as soon as possible. If you allow them to continue without a consequence, in their minds, you're telling them it's ok. If they're breaking a rule or even getting close to breaking one, be sure to talk to them about it. Make sure they're learning the difference between you overlooking a mistake as opposed to them thinking that there is no consequence to their actions.

My husband and I found ourselves frustrated about our kids not following instructions. They were waiting until the third or fourth time they were told to even move. We found ourselves constantly issuing consequences and, at one point, fussing, nagging, and yelling. That kind of stuff wears you out mentally and emotionally. Do you find yourself saying things like,

"Lord, why won't these kids *just listen?*!

I want kids who do what I say *the first time*!

Why do I have to say something *a million* times before anything gets done?!"

The answer is actually pretty simple. First, look at the adult's behavior. Are the adults self-motivated? Do the adults delay in getting things done? I know there were a ton of things I needed to do that I kept putting off for whatever reason. So how could I complain about them doing it? I needed to clean up my act. However, before I entered into the self-bashing stage, I recalled Romans 8:1

There is therefore now no condemnation for those who are in Christ Jesus. KJV

When I considered that, I realized that I needed to forgive myself and my kids. That didn't mean we didn't need to correct their behavior (and mine as well), but to move forward, forgiveness needed to occur.

What was the answer to my second question? I clearly heard the words of my mother, "If you want your child to listen the first time, correct them the first time." Before you jump out there, you must have a plan for how you'll handle potential situations and responses. Just because you decide to take a turn doesn't mean they'll follow along! Remember, if you haven't been keeping your word, you've essentially altered the overall trust in the household. In other words, if they know you'll take 20 minutes when you said it would be 5, don't expect them to fall in line when you adjust your behavior. That goes both ways. Be patient with them because you've been letting them get away with it for a while.

Another key action is implementation. If you talk to them and issue a consequence the first time, there would be no second or third time (so no blowing up). It will teach them to do what they are told the first time. Old school parents really had it down. The first time you did something wrong, you got a clear indication that you should *never* do it again. It may have seemed strict at the time, but it got the job done!

The third answer came through Scripture as well.

Death and life are in the power of the tongue: and they that love it shall eat the fruit thereof. Proverbs 18:21

You have a choice. You can say words that cause things to grow or to die. What you say affects those around you. We've all experienced it. We'll call a good friend to hear uplifting words. We avoid people that always speak negative words. We know that hurtful words do more to discourage than to encourage, so we should watch our words. Did you ever hear, "Watch your mouth" as a child? There was a reason. Our elders knew that when you say something long enough and believe it, it will happen.

As a parent, I had to admit, I'd been saying all kinds of off the wall comments and, in some way, believing it. You know, crazy stuff like: "Lord, these kids are driving me crazy", "Y'all have all lost your minds", "You little people are crazy!" So what was the state of our house? Crazy. Not all the time, but the more I said it, the more it would manifest. How did it stop? I stopped ranting and started being more selective with my words.

Finally, take a look at your buttons. You know, the ones people push to get a reaction out of you. One thing about kids is that they learn how to get their way, and it starts from birth. Babies cry. Toddlers use tantrums. School-aged kids' tactics range from crying or stomping to moping and complaining. Sometimes it's to express their emotions, but sometimes it's to push your buttons to get you to spring into action.

On the other end of the stick are the parents. It's not fair to you to be in an environment where your buttons are constantly being pushed. Home is an environment that you do have control over. So take time to figure out what your triggers are and diffuse them (or at least set up barriers around them until you do). If you know that dirty dishes are your pet peeve, set up the chore schedule to give plenty of time for them to be done before you arrive. Lay out the consequence clearly for them not being done. For example, if your child gets home at 3:30 and you arrive home at 5:30, tell them to have it done by the time you get home. If not, they'll lose privileges (upcoming activities, something they're expecting to receive or access to something they like to do). It's your house. Run it!

Finally, let's destroy this "I'll keep doing it until I get caught, or something really bad happens" mentality. We watch the news and see how embezzlement, infidelity, robbery, fraud, and murder are revealed daily. Let's stop that way of thinking in our kids. It only ends in disaster.

Never Reward Bad Behavior

Temper tantrums? Throwing things across the room? Hitting or Biting? Silent treatment? Moping or pouting? Cursing or being disrespectful? Never reward that kind of behavior. Don't try to butter them up, nudge them or pay them to come out of their funk. Don't cave because you can't take the silence. Use the silence to reevaluate the situation, and be sure you made the right decision or took the right course of action. The biggest thing is this: let them get over it. Allow them time and space to deal with their feelings, and when they're ready, they'll come out of it. Giving them fake compliments, money, toys, candy, or their way only teaches them how to manipulate YOU. Once they find your button, they'll become pros at pushing it. This method also works with adults (try it at work and see how people respond).

Got a Kid Who's Always Dragging?

Before you consider a consequence, make sure that there's nothing physically, emotionally, or otherwise wrong. Some kids are early risers or may shut down after a certain point of the day. But if you have a true turtle in human form, consider using this clever trick. If you're last, you clean up after everyone else. This goes for mealtime, cleanup time after playing, homework time, etc. *You can also use this trick for the speed demons who try to get there first so they can get dibs on everything. Have them help set the table, pour drinks, get napkins, or wipe down the counters. They can even help cook!

Greedy?

One of my pet peeves of preteen boys is being greedy. Not being hungry, but all-out greedy! Eating is a blessing in this country, not a sport! Yeah, I know there are competitions for eating, but you know what I'm talking about. My oldest would think it was so cool to come home after eating with his friends and tell how he ate eight slices of pizza or ate four burgers (plus fries, drink, and dessert). There's nothing funny, cool, or safe about that! So, what to do? Well, I made him eat only roughage every mean for the next day or so to clean him out, and that was also my prompting to have him learn another level of cooking skills! When a child understands what goes into preparing a meal, they're less compelled to wolf it down or be wasteful.

Here are other methods:

Teach them to C-H-E-W! I think the ratio of chews to swallows was 15 to 1 or 30 to 1 (it depends who you ask).

Let them eat more to fill up, but it must be veggies. Or give them high protein and high fiber options, like nuts. They are great sources of nutrition without breaking the bank!

Allow them to drink while eating, or even before eating.

Our house has a staunch rule for eating first, then drinking. With a teen, I learned to let him (or even require him) to drink a cup of milk or water before eating. He plays basketball, so he needs all the water and calcium he can get! Not to mention the huge difference we saw in the increase of his height (and shoe size) as well as the decrease in our grocery bill. Boys can be locusts!

Body or Room Odor

I have two sons, and they are completely different in this area. The oldest could choke a yak with the smell, but the younger could go 3-5 days before he had the slightest odor. Weird. Anyway, I've found that sometimes there's no getting around it…boys can STINK! I mean, not normal stink. Clutch your nose and mouth like you got hit by a brick _STINK_. Did I mention they can't smell it? I made one of them go in the hall, shut the door, count to ten, and walk back in. What did he smell? "Nothing." I think his nostrils fell out the frame or just gave up the fight. There's no other logical explanation! Anyway, here are some tips for getting rid of boy stink. These are some ideas for body odor:

Go back to the basics. Yeah, this is the down and dirty. Ask yourself (and them) the following:

Are they washing properly? You may have to revisit the overall process. Some kids don't make enough lather. Some don't wash their entire body. If they're not getting every crack and crevice, that's bad. If they're not "hitting the hot spots", that's really bad!

Are they using a fresh washcloth every few days?

Is the washcloth hung up and allowed to dry in between uses? Otherwise, they're washing with bacteria from it sitting around wet.

Do they pre-wash their washcloth before each use?)Do they wet their washcloth, soap it up, rinse it out, then lather to actually wash their body?)

Do they have a washcloth just for their face? This is my personal preference-tub cloth and sink cloth (don't wash your face with the cloth you're using to clean your nether regions! *Eeeeeew*!!)

Do they rinse all the soap off? Soap actually *loosens* dirt. Unless you use antibacterial soap or a cleanser with antibacterial properties, you're not killing germs, just lifting germs and dirt. If you don't rinse it away, you're walking around with it on your skin.

Are they drying properly? Wet areas left in the dark (pits and crotch) create stinkiness.

Are they washing at the appropriate time of day? Night showers are great, but if they sweat in their sleep or rarely wash their sheets, they're gonna be stinky.

Are they putting on deodorant or antiperspirant? There are natural ones that work very well, too.

Is there something going on hormonally? They may need to be checked out by a doctor.

My all-time favorite:

Are they getting enough water? If your system isn't being flushed out daily, you stink. No matter how old you are. It'll come out in your sweat, urine, skin, whatever, but it'll come out. If they stink, I'd honestly try increasing their water as well as the other steps mentioned.

The following are ideas to use if his laundry is already being done regularly, and the odor still lingers.

Build up your arsenal. Air fresheners, odor neutralizers, timed sprayers, scented oils, and plug-in heated candle scents may work.

If not, you're in the big leagues. Move on to 13-17.

Baking soda can be used on floors and beds for 30 mins up to a few hours then vacuumed up to remove some odors.

Shampooing the carpet and washing the curtains may help.

Spray with a 50/50 vinegar and water solution.

Place a potpourri pouch specially designed for air filters inside the vent in the room.

Rent a flame thrower and torch his room. Be sure to remove any living creatures (or siblings) first! Then throw him out to live in the wild.

Ok, just kidding about the last part!

Sloppiness

One "quick" way to stop this habit is to have the child

to repeat the task until it's done right. This will mean observing the child doing the task and finding the root of the issue. When I was a kid, I couldn't turn in messy handwriting. I had to rewrite the entire document over if there were messy eraser marks, poor handwriting, smudges, or tears in the paper. It taught me to take my time, be careful, and try your best to get it right the first time, so you don't have to do it over and over. I hold on to that belief to this day! My husband had the same philosophy taught in his household. I'll never forget the story he told us about the term "semicircular canals". He had a school paper to write about it, and because he kept messing it up, he ended up staying up until 2 am redoing it. He was raised in a military family (as was I), so sloppiness and laziness were not tolerated.

I think a great method of correcting handwriting is to go back to the basics. Pull out some handwriting paper. Even pull out the tracing ones if you need to! My oldest is on the brink of going that route (don't tell him! I want it to be a surprise). His handwriting isn't really bad, it's just at the cusp of being bad. I'd prefer he get it under control before I have to intervene. If you decide to use the handwriting paper method, make a bunch of copies before you start. Or you could laminate them (that's really great if you're using the ones for tracing). Doing this practice may help them get that handwriting in a more legible state. Side note: I'm a math professor. Many kids don't see why their handwriting is a big deal. One of the challenges that kids have is understanding that good handwriting is more for others than it is for themselves. So it's important for them to know that if no one can read what they wrote, no one can discover their brilliance. If that doesn't sell, tell them they can only have jacked up handwriting if they're going to be a doctor when they grow up! Just kidding. Try to convince them to fix their writing because (as we all know from school), if the teacher can't read it, they can't grade it (or you'll get a zero)!

Blurters

Blurting can be great-in the proper time and place. In open mic (when you're the one <u>on</u> the mic), it's great! In class, not so much. I saw a pin on Pinterest that said, "Before you say something, T.H.I.N.K. first. Is it TRUE? Is it HELPFUL? Is it INSPIRING? Is it NECESSARY? Is it KIND? Before you correct, find out the reason for the blurting. Does the child feel they're not being heard or understood? Do they want to be a part of the group? Do they want to make sure they're on the right track with their thinking? Are they lonely and want attention? Does their thinking process work better when they speak aloud? Consider these things before issuing a correction. Discussing time and place may be the key to modifying the behavior. Discussing their emotional state and acknowledging their feelings by affirming that they are valued and loved may solve the problem. You don't want them to stop participating (as a teacher, I've seen how using the wrong method of "correcting" this behavior can actually stunt a student's academic & emotional growth), you just want to be sure that they know when and how to express themselves in a way that is beneficial to everyone in earshot.

Not Washing Hands

I have two sons. They love to play outside. They used to come in and act like they washed their hands. We used to go back and forth about it two and three times a day. I got tired of the fight, so you know what I did? I put some obnoxious smelling soap in the soap dispensers they use! That stuff was so loud that when they came anywhere near, I could smell it! That put a halt to me accusing them (and sometimes being wrong) about hand washing. For some reason, they liked the smell of it and started doing it without me reminding them. Who knows, maybe the answer all along was giving them a scent they liked!

Mind-Numbingly Noisy

Some kids are tappers, drummers, hummers, buzzers, or squealers. My middle child is a squeaker/squealer. He can make the highest, most piercing sound you ever heard. It's usually when someone is chasing or tickling him. This can be quite often because he's a perfect target. He's a little short for his age and a little small, too. Don't call DSS on me. It's hereditary. Poor thing, he gets it from my Dad and my husband! So we don't expect him to get much taller for a while. Anyway, it's been the hardest thing to get him to stop that squealing. He still does it, but he's gotten much better about respecting time and place. Outside is ok, inside is not! I read somewhere that a lady made her sons listen to the Barney theme song for 10 minutes if they went overboard with the crazy sound effects and noises!

Safety Word

If your child is getting out of line (noises, actions, comments, etc.), create a safety word to let them know to cut it out. This will keep them (and you) from the embarrassment of calling them out in public. It can also serve as a warning before having to take further action to correct the behavior. Be sure it's a word that's not degrading or embarrassing because no one should know other than you and your child.

Stomping

Come up with a creative consequence for stomping. Some suggest making them do it for a longer time, like a minute. I can see how that would work. If I had to stomp my feet for more than a few seconds, I think I'd get the point and stop completely!

For small children, you may be able to get away using the game 1-2-3 Red Light. Kid Law dictates that you must stop when you hear "1-2-3 Red Light". The purpose is for the child to get themselves together mentally or emotionally. Then the parent feels they have, they call "green light". My husband's mom made him do that to stop him from stomping. It worked!

Fits and Temper Tantrums

Fits and temper tantrums don't fly in my house. I tell my kids they have to take that mess outside or to their room and do it quietly. You can be mad, but you're not gonna punish everyone else with the noise. Kids are due to express their feelings, but not at everyone else's expense. Let them go and blow off steam and rejoin the group when they're done. We also let them know if they want to talk about their feelings after they finish venting, the family will be ready to listen. So they know we care about their problem and their feelings, but not the other foolishness and carrying on. Let's face it. Our society feeds kids to have an audience to obnoxious behavior. Think about every reality show you've seen, the news and movies…yeah. Foolishness=audience. Not in our house!

An idea my husband implemented is what he calls "pillow talk". It's not what we adults think of pillow talk, but it's when a child is upset and goes to their room to say what is on their mind into their pillow. That way, they don't disrespect anyone with harsh words, they're not screaming and disruptive, but they get a release for their emotions.

Playing Dumb

Sorry for the terminology (I know "dumb" is a bad word), but I'm calling it what it is. You know how your child is sent to do something, and they do it halfway like they don't know what the job calls for? Some kids do it to get out of the task. They know someone will come along, fuss about it for a bit, do it for them, and then they're off the hook. Boys (and some men I know) are notorious for it. Those who have roots in the South know the saying: If you did it half-a**ed, you didn't <u>do</u> it at all! Well, my kids have it rough. If they don't do it right the first time, they have to do it over until they do it right. Sometimes they get the lecture to go along with it. It goes like this: now wouldn't it just be quicker to do it right the first time instead of having to do it over and over until you do it right? It may seem like torture, but it'll teach them to be more detail-oriented and careful about their work. That's a life skill! Don't agree? Think about how many times paperwork or processes have to be redone because someone didn't do their job right the first time. Think about the delay it causes and all the money wasted (or the amount it costs taxpayers)!

Unnecessary Questions

Does your child constantly ask you questions they should (or already) know the answer to? This can range from "Do I have to do my homework?", "Do I have to go to bed?", "Can I have some water?", "Where is the TV remote?", "How do you spell ____?" Instead of answering them (and driving yourself crazy), say <u>nothing</u>. Make them think it through or figure it out for themselves. My mom used to send me to the dictionary every time I asked her how to spell something. When I asked, "How can I look it up if I can't spell it?" she'd (in the beginning stages of my learning to spell more difficult words) tell me to sound it out and keep trying until I found it. I learned to also use the phonetic spelling in the dictionary. The result? A spelling bee winner! Yep! I'm a very good speller. Now definitions? Forget about it!! But in general, I tell my kids that if I have to get up and do it, find it or explain it, they'll have to do a chore from the chore can to pay me back. That usually ends that.

Sneaking Snacks?

First, are you feeding them?! Ok, I just had to say that (gave me a good laugh). I apologize. I assume that you're feeding them healthy food in the right portion at consistent times of the day. I also assume you're tracking or observing when their growth spurts occur. However, one idea is to ditch the cookie jar. Leave the cookies in the super noisy wrapper so you can hear the little culprits!

Some parents opt for a locked pantry. Some ditch sweet snacks altogether! I refuse to get rid of all my sweet snacks (hey, a Mom's gotta have something for herself). I give them a number limit and have my kids brush their teeth after every single sweet snack. By sweet snacks, it could be candy, cookies, juice, or gum. My husband piggybacks and says, "Rot your teeth out on your own insurance!" Sometimes we make them drink milk or 2 cups of water after. So we don't deny them, because it'll just make them want it more. Yet they've gotta know there are parameters and they need to take care of their bodies. Not to mention, they have to eat their veggies if they want to see a single snack.

In researching this issue, people are putting alarms on their fridges, taking doors off their kids' rooms, giving consequences for eating sweets, etc. I won't speak to those. That's your choice. However, one thing that works for us when they're becoming junk-food junkies is to put the sweets out of reach and put out a bowl of fruit and pre-cut fruits and veggies in the fridge. They swarm them like locusts and lay off the sweets. Somewhat. Out of sight out of mind is true. My husband and I have a specific spot we call "the stash" where we keep stuff we want to preserve. It could be anything that we want to be sure we'll actually get a taste of (when kids hit growth spurts, they'll eat carpet, hubcaps, shoes, whatever). Our stash has rules, though. If a spouse ever discloses the location and/or contents of "the stash" to a child, they lose all rights and privileges to "the stash" and all future stashes! It's severe, but in marriage, it's supposed to be us against the world, babe! Ok, in all seriousness, set guidelines, parameters, and plans A-E at least. Oh yeah, one last tip. You may want to have them drink a cup of milk at the beginning of snack (or if they're old enough, let them drink before or during the meal) so they won't be as ravenous for sweets.

Solving Sibling Disputes

Today was rough. My middle is fighting with the oldest and the youngest. They are always fighting over who gets to play with him. I keep telling them he's not a puppy or a toy. You can't *make* someone play with you! Anyway, today I think I had a breakthrough. I had to get the middle child alone and have a heart-to-heart. I gave him "permission" to be a man and make his own decision about who he'd play with and when. He didn't have to play with someone even if they wanted him to. So didn't have to respond to being called from one room to another. He could also just be by himself. A wave of relief came across his face.

I also shared with him about wanting to "run away from home" for a little bit just to be alone. Sometimes I wanted to take him, Daddy, his brother, or his sister. Whoever understood me the most at the moment. His face brightened at that (he really understood that one!) and said, "Yeah, me too." We closed the situation with an agreement that he could put his foot down and that he could come play with me whenever he wanted to.

Next, I had to get the other two to get a grip! Especially my oldest. I have a belief that if you get them out of the house to play with kids their own age, the arguments will decrease. Mathematically, it's gotta be right because they won't *be* there to argue as much! Anyway, we had to review the Golden Rule. So after a good "put the shoe on the other foot" discussion, he calmed down and saw it through his brother and sister's eyes. My daughter was satisfied because she always catches it from her oldest brother. The height disadvantage doesn't help her case, either. She'll be right as rain, but because she's the youngest and smallest, he thinks he's always right. *Side note: this part of parenthood is not easy. I know sometimes I should take my husband's approach ("they're siblings, that's what they do, if they kill each other we can finally get a decent meal"). However, mommies don't like to hear their babies fight! So the next time they get into it, I think I'll go shopping. I may say it's for groceries, but I have a feeling the store will be out of what I was looking for, and my breath will smell suspiciously of Rocky Road and Daiquiri Ice ice cream!

General Disobedience, Disrespect, Or Defiance (A.K.A. Lost Their Durn Mind!)

When this happens (it inevitably does), my kids have to hit the chore can. Sometimes they may have to apologize or do chores for the person they disrespected, or they may lose some privileges. Sometimes, I pull out the big guns. I call it the ridiculous list. It's the stuff that's so crazy that they decide IMMEDIATELY to NEVER, EVER, EVER MAKE THAT CHOICE AGAIN. See 20 ideas below:

Disinfect everyone's shoes (if ANYONE plays sports, this is an awful thing to do!)

Wash Daddy's work clothes for the week (gag!)

Clean <u>under</u> the fridge drawers

Give Daddy a foot massage

Pull weeds out of the garden, yard or flowerbed

Clean the fish tank

Clean the gutters

Clean the big trash cans (the ones you take to the curb)

Get the cobwebs out of the corners

Clean out the oven

Iron everyone's clothes for the week

Vacuuming out the kitchen drawers

Clean out the junk drawer

Clean the kitchen or dining room chairs with the carpet shampooer

Clean out the garage

Clean the fireplace

Clean ALL glass in the house

Clean under all couch cushions

De-poop the yard

De-poop the neighbor's yard

You get quiet kids, a clean house, and no complaints of boredom!

Being a math teacher, I know one of the most undervalued tactics that a parent can use are steps and repetition. I think a lot more would get done correctly if we stuck to the steps and did it over and over until we got it right. I've tried on many counts to utilize this bit of wisdom with my children and found that I was failing, Not for lack of effort, but lack of clarity and/or persistence. Now, in my own defense, I am outmanned. My husband and I have three kids who are smart. Very smart. Those little jokers know how to wear us down! They don't win about much, but when they find a crack in the door, look out! Even my mother tried to tell me, "You've got some brilliant kids. Kids are always smarter than you." At first, I was offended. Honestly, I was a bit ticked off! Then I realized, she meant that as a generalization for *all* parents. Think about it. You're teaching them the best you've got! Their energy is fresh out of the package, and you're gearing down because you're closer to being 80 than they are. So, how can you possibly win? One word: WISDOM.

The best battles have been won using wisdom. It doesn't matter if you're outnumbered, out-skilled, or outsmarted. If you can use the wisdom you've accrued over the years, you've got 'em beat! Think about it. How many times has your kid done the exact opposite of what you told them? Well, tell them to do the exact opposite of what you want! Even babies seem to come into the world doing that. Sleeping during the day and up all night. Your job is to be observant, then use their behavior patterns to guide them toward the desired behavior. Now, if you have kids like mine, they're so literal that it can sometimes drive you up the wall. So be careful! Don't say what you don't mean if they can't handle it. Don't be general if they need specifics.

Case in point, today I finally made myself stop and create a chore can. It's not for behavior modification (well, not at first), it's so I don't have to keep writing their chores down under their name and erasing it every day. I just refuse to let them wear me out before they have to live on their own! Here's how I did it: I took note cards and cut them into squares. On one side, I wrote the name of the chore. For example, "steam mop the floors". On the back, I wrote which rooms and that the floors must be vacuumed first (if they weren't, you have to do that chore too). Finally, refill the steam mop and put it back in the pantry.

Now, I can tell any one of them "steam mop the floor" and they know what I mean, but I want to leave as little margin for error as possible. Also, only my oldest has been released to do this chore. When the other two hit that milestone, they would've seen the card and description enough times to know what it takes.

I also put the chores into categories. Some are so trivial that you must choose another chore. So big jobs have only the job name on the front (like vacuum upstairs or clean the tub), smaller jobs (put away small dishes, couch pillows) have been paired up so that you put in a good 10-20 minutes of work. Still, others require an adult to be present (clean out the fridge or clean out junk drawer). Oh, and if a few jobs get too much attention because the kids purposely are choosing them (this happens sometimes even though I make mine pull blindly), just take the overused cards out for a few days!

I saw something somewhere a few years ago (clarity

just went out the window, ha!) about taking the wiggle room out for kids when giving them chore assignments. This dad decided that in every room, he'd post how to do the chore step by step. He'd write something like:

Clean the kitchen <u>means</u>:

Remove all items from counters

Wipe down countertops with wet wipes

Put all items back

Sweep floors

Take out the trash (if trash day, pull bin to the curb) and replace the trash bag

Fill water pitcher

Mop floor

Clean the sink with cleanser and rinse thoroughly

and so on. I almost fell out of my chair! I'd had this fight with my oldest for years. Even he and his dad were constantly discussing, "Is your room *your* idea of clean, or is it *Daddy* clean?" Then my husband would go into specifics about what "Daddy clean" entailed. Every…single…time!

I was just sooo tired of it!! So we looked at how the household was running. If we were in business, would our way of "handling our employees" work? Nope. So we came up with some basics. Be clear, have consequences for infractions. Now, to be honest, we're not big on rewards. We are constantly doing something for/with our kids, so I feel like we're just collecting on what we've already paid out. Don't get me wrong, they aren't spoiled (our kids started doing chores the moment they were old enough to fold), but we can get slack sometimes about making them walk the line consistently. Then we have to "retrain". It's a vicious cycle. Don't follow in our footsteps on that one.

So, back to what we did. We made the cards for the chore can and then we also made an infraction list. Well, it's more like a discipline sheet. If you do XYZ, then ABC will happen. For example, if you skip out on your chore, you have to do everyone else's. Not rocket science, either do one chore or do five! The infraction is also put on the family calendar. Once, my daughter decided she'd be slick and play with molding dough on the carpet when Mommy had *just* said she could only play with it at the table. Well, when she was busted, she lost her privileges with the dough for seven days. Seem harsh? Ok. But she has *never, ever* done it since! No yelling, no spanking, nothing but remorse for her own actions.

That was great for my youngest, but the middle child would have weaseled his way out of that one somehow. So, I have to tap into his mental motivations. As opposed to taking something away, he is one who has to understand why his infraction was a bad decision. He's the one who is emotionally analytical (I probably just made that term up-I really don't know). If we can literally talk some sense into him, he's not likely to make the mistake again. Or if he does, he'll hang his head about it. He also punishes himself by going into his room and pouting until he stops beating himself up about it. So, not too much work there. Shoot, I don't have to punish him or even raise my voice. Usually, I only have to raise an eyebrow for him to know he's crossed the line.

If it was only that easy with my pre-teen. The "Outhinker". I remember when I was a kid I'd get in trouble for two things: thinking too much or not thinking enough. It felt like walking a tightrope. As a parent, I feel like I'm the tightrope walking instructor. It's CRAZY!!! What used to work was asking, "How would you feel if someone did that to you?" Teens don't always care. They are just about them, what they want, how they feel, blah blah blah. Well, I do have one leg up. I used to teach pre-teens. The biggest thing that works for them is discipline. The consequence chart was for this one. He needed to see a clear cut description of how what he did would cause an outcome. Now it's up to him-no excuses. Oh yeah, don't forget to put a consequence for whining, pouting, cursing (God forbid that's going on), throwing things, hurting others, etc. for however far the barometer runs in your house. If your situation is very serious (the last three mentioned or worse), consider other options like summer with Grandma, boot camp, military school, or whatever the situation takes. I've had parents who had to threaten their kids with signing them over to the state, adoption, kicking them out, etc. And also look into the laws in your area.

Some help parents out, while others seem to take away every bit of power needed to raise a halfway decent kid!

My secret weapon of choice? PRAYER. Usually, it goes something like, "Lord, that is <u>YOUR</u> child. Please talk to them before I have to" or "Father, get your child!" or some other stuff I dare not put into print (I'm not stupid). But it never fails, the situation is handled, and my hair and blood pressure remain intact. Usually, when I pray, God is quick to remind me of what I did as a child (or a few days ago, whichever is the case) and how He forgave me for it. I'm still His child, and I'm still messing up, and He has never stopped loving me for a single moment. That reminder usually gets me through. Or their dad will come in and set them straight. Works either way for me! Prayer has a 100% success rate. You can also read to them from the Bible or give them a scripture to read on their own. I've included some of those as well (check the prayer index). Some kids get it right away, and for some, it takes a while to sink in. Some have to mess up a while, and then the light bulb comes on. Bottom line, we as parents want our kids to understand why their behavior is incorrect and teach them to modify it before more serious consequences come along.

Soapbox time again: I'll never understand why there are laws in place that leave parents helpless to discipline their children, but after a certain age authorities can spray them with mace, unleash dogs on them, handcuff them and beat them with sticks the size of my forearm! A friend of mine told me that a law enforcement officer said if her child (a teenager between 15 and 17) went into a drug house, she couldn't go in to get her because it was her daughter's choice and the parent would be trespassing! The police *knew* it was a drug house!! So be sure to check the laws in your area.

6 LIFE PRESERVERS
TIPS FOR OTHER HOT TOPICS

Prayer Index

Sometimes I go straight to the Word of God. There are scriptures about how to be loving, caring, diligent, compliant, merciful, submissive, honest, a leader, protection, knowing a true friend, and more in the Bible. Quite a few are in the book of Proverbs. The Gospels of Matthew, Mark, Luke, and John have a ton as well. The fight about what is right or wrong isn't mine. It's right there in black and white (red and white if Jesus said it), so there's no argument. I don't use the Bible to beat my kids down, condemn them, or make them feel ashamed. It's to remind them of the choices they have in life and the outcome of those choices. It also makes it very clear that they don't have to make those choices on their own. God loves them and put these reminders there just for them because of that immense love.

If your kids don't have the opportunity to attend children's church (not all churches have it), consider taking them to a church that does, or AWANA, Vacation Bible School, or to a church who has Wednesday night Bible Study for kids. We used to drop our kids off to AWANA and then go to adult Bible Study at our home church. It worked wonders! They refuse to throw away their AWANA books, badges, and awards. They actually witness to other kids. Their teachers are so grateful because ours don't cause problems in class (*usually*-they're still kids). If you want to find an AWANA chapter near you, visit AWANA.org for locations and more details.

Naptime

I polled some parents, and they gave some great ideas for getting your child settled in for nap time or bedtime. Here are a few that were noteworthy:

No TV, video games or high stimulation 30 minutes before bed/nap time (very effective! Gears the mind down before turning in)

Take a walk for 10-15 minutes, then home for a warm bath or shower

A warm shower 10-20 minutes before bed

25-50 jumping jacks before bed

Lavender lotion rub-down

Lavender oils for the tub (or shower) before bed

Backrub (my Grandma did this, and it knocked us out every time!!)

Classical music (only during nap/bedtime)

Put them to bed with a nature cd or near a small fountain

Tuck them in really tight

Feed them a higher carb meal (not <u>every</u> night, just if they've been restless a few nights in a row)

A warm glass of milk (make sure it's a <u>small</u> glass, or you'll have a different problem)

Separate siblings to adjoining rooms and sit where you can view both until they fall off to sleep (move them back to their room if they're sound sleepers)

Deep breathing (it really works!)

Counting sheep

Making a palette on the floor (pillows, blankets, etc.)

Graham crackers, bananas and a small cup of milk

Chamomile tea (a small cup or two)

Tuck them in under heavy blankets (Grandmas used this trick, and it WORKED!)

My mother's trick: "You don't have to take a nap. Just go lay across your bed for 10 minutes." Worked every time (NOTE: make sure there's no clock in their room. It may not work for those clock-watching types)!

The biggest challenge may be to find out (or remember) what works for each child. For me, I had to recall when they were babies. Whatever worked then still works now. The oldest is a heavy sleeper by nature. Now I have to get through the preteen, "I'm too old for naps" mess. He pouts, whines, drags, and then falls asleep within 5 minutes. The middle child needs a good, thorough cuddle and some monitoring. I have to stay there for 5-10 minutes before he'll give in and go to sleep (but those heavy blankets help a lot-he feels comforted). The youngest? Please! She's like her Mommy. If she's tired, she'll leave and go to bed. Sometimes she'll even announce it. Sometimes we're looking around for her, and she's already grabbed her blankie and is on her bed (or some random place) knocked out drooling!

So, learn your kids. Try different things. It may be one of the things I mentioned, or you may have to put them in the car and go for a drive. Either way, your sanity is worth the cost of gas! If all else fails, drop them off to a drop-in daycare so *YOU* can get a nap. Sometimes it's not them. It's *you* who needs a nap!

Quiet Time

This one is GOLD, people! You must have quiet time.

Whether a set time of day or not, be sure to create it, explain it, and enforce it. It helps your kids calm themselves and find something to do that will allow you time to get some things done. Now, this also means you'll have to check-in. We all know quiet + kids = suspicion! However, if you can get them to do it, your entire family wins. Right now, for instance, I've brought all three of my children downstairs. Why? Because playing with their wrestling men (and doing whatever my daughter was doing) just got too noisy. So what are they doing? Sitting on the floor quietly until I think they've gotten the point. If that doesn't work, they'll be hitting the chore can. What's another good reason for quiet time? To let them know that their noise level affects others in the house and to help them take responsibility and control their volume. Soapbox again: when did elementary schools stop teaching and enforcing inside/outside voice?! Sheesh!

"The Box"

Tired of telling your child to pick up after themselves (like a million times)? Don't!! Just pick it up and toss it in The Box. What's The Box, you ask? It's one of my favorite, newly found treasures. This is a plastic 13-gallon storage tub (like the ones you store in the attic) that I use to hold the kids' stuff hostage in. They have to pull a chore out of the chore can (or sometimes they volunteer or ask what they need to do) to get it back. You determine how long to keep their items in there. *Don't lug the whole system, take the memory card, cords, controllers, or anything else that's critical for the game to work. Grab those critical components to the game and stash them for a bit to get your point across. It doesn't have to be for grounding. It can be for discipline for picking up after themselves.

Cleanup Games

-Give them a small amount of money for every day they keep their room clean. I would not suggest starting with folding money. Then again, if you have boys, you may want to try it. Boys usually want a toy or game that's a bit out of their budget. You can help them by tallying up their days as credit toward what they want (using a calendar may help keep track). So if they want a $20 item, they need to keep their room clean for 20 days. Or whatever you decide. You can go 25 cents or 50 cents or $2 a day. However, you choose. The point is, they get the incentive and you get a clean room.

 Side note: our house rule is that your bedroom must be cleaned by 7 pm each night. This allows me to check it, see when laundry needs to be done, etc. when we kiss them goodnight. It also cuts down on the morning rat race of "I can't find…", "Mommy, have you seen my…" and my favorite, "I don't have any more…"

-Play the "who can clean their room faster" game between siblings. You may have to throw in an incentive like they get to ride up front on the next outing, control the radio in the car or pick next location to go out to eat.

-Hide money in their room and tell them it's their reward

for cleaning it up. Mix it up a bit and put $1 in quarters! So they have to find all four. It teaches them that it "pays" to clean up their room!

-Tell them to find something in their room (that you've already removed), and they must put things away until they find it.

Unselfishness

One thing that I've learned as a parent is that the million written and unwritten rules in society that we usually make an effort to abide by deal with selflessness. If you think about the laws of the land, most of them are in place to help others. Why do we have speed limits? So we don't hurt anyone or ourselves. Why do we use turn signals? To let the other person know what we're about to do. Why do we push our chairs in after getting up? So it's not in the way, and so the area looks neat and tidy. If you sprinkle when you tinkle, why are you a sweetie and wipe the seatie? So the next person won't have to. So you can see, it's not about us. It's about everyone else. That's what life should be about-looking out for others. And that's what the basic rules we teach our children (sharing, taking turns, being nice, taking care of what you're given and encouraging) are all about.

Think about the stuff you're frustrated about with parenting. Nine times out of ten, it'll be something stemming from selfishness. Not cleaning up after themselves, dragging when it's time to go, not pitching in, breaking curfew, abusing their bodies, etc. It is a result of not taking other's feelings into consideration.

So how do we teach this habit? Yes, selflessness is a habit (even though some have compassion like it's a gift). Start very early. When they can say "mine", it's too late. The fact that they know this term is an indication that they are looking out for themselves, right? Using words like "ours", "share", etc. help children understand that they're important. Also, share. Share a lot. Share meals, chores, family time, outings, money, take turns, etc. Don't complain while you're doing it. Do a great job of showing a team effort. Make it fun. Create a goal. If we work together and complete the task without complaining for ___ days, we'll all _____ together. Share thoughts on how many days it should be and what the reward will be. Change it up every so often, so everyone's ideas are used. For example, if the family keeps the kitchen clean as a team for seven days straight, go out for ice cream together as a family reward! If you keep it clean a month, do a movie night. Do it for six months and go on a weekend vacation. Change the time frame and reward to suit your family. Show it pays to work together without complaining.

Help Them Make the Connection

Calmly explain why taking out the trash, washing dishes, cleaning their room, cutting the grass, and mopping the floors is good for the entire family. It's not always about keeping the house smelling good or being neat and tidy, but it's about health, having room to play, and keeping critters from invading your territory. It also helps us to work as a team, reach a common goal, and spend time together. Not to mention that it's good exercise, a stress reliever, and a good time to talk to your family members.

Side note: While writing this section of the book, I got distracted. Two of my children began screaming about a spider. Before running to their aid, I decided to listen a bit. Their father was, in fact, a few feet away, so there was no real need for me to move. However, it wasn't the spider that got me up. It was the scenario. My husband hates, detests, loathes, absolutely despises spiders. However, once again, he's hunting one down and killing it. Why? I finally figured it out. First, some background. I married a neat freak. A military family raised, bounce quarters off the sheets, neat freak. Which is ok, because I'm an organizer and a straightener (my mom was military, too). So we have a balanced household in that category. But, it drives me crazy for him to fuss about certain things. One is crumbs. We have *three* kids. Crumbs are inevitable. So what's the big stinking deal? Well, much to my shame, I must admit that today I finally made a simple connection. Why do we have spiders? We don't have bugs (ants, roaches, other creepy crawlies), but we have spiders. But what do spiders eat? Bugs. What do bugs eat? Crumbs. So why do we have spiders? They're eating the bugs drawn by the ding dang *crumbs*!!! Yeeeesh!!!! You've gotta be kidding me!

Why am I telling you all this? I'm telling you all this because even the simplest connections can be overlooked.

Sometimes you really need to spell things out step by step. Don't get me wrong. I'm no dummy. Shoot, I teach MATH! But I really missed the boat on this one because I never thought it through (I just thought my husband was upset because he just wanted the house tidy). It was really about keeping all those within it healthy and happy.

Nip Entitlement in the Bud

This generation is something else. They want everything. Free. Yesterday! Oh yeah, did I mention they want <u>you</u> to pay for it, no questions asked, and be primed and ready for their next request? In my day, you didn't ask for money for anything other than the ice cream truck before the age of 10. You asked to go out to play! You asked for some more to eat. You could ask to go somewhere or for someone to come over, but you didn't fix your mouth to ask for money unless it was for something important. Also, you had better buy what you said it was for. You could ask for a toy around your birthday or Christmas or around report card time (those grades <u>better</u> be right!), and that was it. We'd dare not ask for clothing or shoes that cost hundreds of dollars, unnecessary gadgets (much less uneducational), or things that would be easily broken or taken for granted. Our parents wanted to instill the positive type of pride that comes from a wage well earned or earning what you wanted, not the peer pressure-driven requests for some new fad item.

We must teach our children to earn their privileges.

Yes, there are some things that they should come to expect because it comes with being a kid, but there's a huge entitlement issue in our country. When I was growing up, chores were done <u>before</u> asking to go outside or asking to turn on the TV. The bed was made, and the room was clean <u>before</u> turning your feet toward the kitchen. You brushed your teeth, combed your hair, and did your chores (for the most part) without being told! Now, it's just a mess. Kids don't see why they have to do anything. Many parents aren't making responsibility a necessity. This is all while the news reports grow more depressing, the employment percentage drops, and the crime rate grows. So let's clear some of this misunderstanding up by my making some connections (the teacher in me just kicked in, so bear with me).

Let's play a game called What Do They Do? By taking this short quiz, you will be able to see the potential for harmful adult behaviors. If you see these tendencies, make corrective action before the resulting behaviors (outlined in parentheses) occur. Keep in mind, this is not a hard and fast list, and the behavior does not always result in the action. *But who wants to take chances?*

When your kid doesn't get their way, what do they do?

Do they throw tantrums? (in adults, called anger issues, outbursts or fits of rage)

Do they throw things or break things? (in adults called the destruction of or vandalizing property)

Do they speak in a hurtful way to others? (in adults it's labeled verbal abuse, slander, etc.)

Do they just take what they want? (theft, embezzlement, stealing)

Do they do their best to try to physically hurt others? (aggravated assault, murder, etc.)

I've taught since 1998, so I've encountered my fair share of children. I also have ended up re-teaching them in middle school and then again in college. So I have seen this first hand. Sometimes children will become what you accept. If you allow certain behaviors when they're kids, those same tendencies remain until adulthood. You have seen it, too. Think about people you've worked with. Think about how they behaved (or are currently behaving) when they don't get their way. Those positive and negative traits were seeds sown and nurtured by their parents. They are living examples of how it may seem cute or harmless when they're children, but if left unchecked, it turns into some very serious stuff. This is not just a negative message, either. Those good traits that we instill do last. They are even more powerful than the negative if we nurture them. Just keep an eye on it and nurture what you want to grow. The time you will invest on nurturing those positive behaviors will more than pay off in the end! So dig your heels in and stay the course!

Money Isn't Everything

This is a very, very important lesson. I've seen too many relationships and lives destroyed because parents taught their children to chase after and serve money (sometimes no matter what). Small children are being taught to ask for money and learn to act out until they get it. Teens are lying around the house, expecting the world, and not even doing chores or doing their best in school. Young adults are entering college with false ideas of what true wealth and value are. They want to go into a field that makes them happy but are tortured by the worry of what their parents will think or do. It's a sad thing to think about. How many artists never came to be because they were told they won't make enough money to live on? How many writers and teachers don't exist because parents say the paycheck isn't large enough? How many doctors have we missed out on because children were pushed into engineering and vice versa? How many good mechanics, service people, and soldiers have we missed out on because parents were afraid to let their kids explore their true passion? That's why you see so many people unhappy in their profession, then changing job tracks to something they enjoy and are good at later in life. We're teaching children to be slaves to money instead of free to explore their gifts, talents, and dreams. Monetarily rich people have been some of the most miserable people I've met in my life. Who is next in line to be miserable? Children who are trying to be like those miserable "rich" people. We must take a step back and teach our children to see what's really important and strive for meaningful futures, not just lucrative ventures.

Encouragement

Praise your kids for doing well, hitting the mark, or meeting your expectations. Receiving no acknowledgment or hearing them say "about time" is no incentive to keep doing what they ask. Give them a hand, a pat on the back, or some other form of encouragement. Everyone needs it. Think about how it would make you feel at work if you actually received praise for your good works! Now treat your child how you'd like to be treated. We do this around our house, and it's such a great feeling to hear one of them take notice of my efforts and say, "Nice work, Mommy. Good job!" It brings a tear to my eye!

Focus on the positive. Highlight good things that happen at dinner time. If you must mention what a bad day you had, at least end it on a high note. Saying things like, "Well, it was rough, but the payoff is that I get to come home to a great family" or "On the bright side, I helped someone through a tough time" or even "I learned to never do that again!" These are great ways to end it on the upswing. Not only does it teach them how to stay positive, but it keeps you in the habit of keeping a good attitude yourself.

Reward good behavior. Kids now want a treat for making their bed, cleaning their room, and doing stuff _they're supposed to do anyway_. I don't believe in that. That's like paying the mailman for bringing the mail. It's his _job_! Anyway, if your child does go above the mark (getting higher grades than expected, maintaining good grades, getting a task right the 3^(rd) time instead of the 5^(th), or even if it's doing their chores without being told or complaining), reward them. It'll teach them that they are important, their efforts don't go unnoticed, and it'll encourage them to continue to reach higher.

Reward Being Nice

Sound crazy? Maybe not. Thieves, murderers, and bombers get more attention on the news these days than those who are making a real effort of doing the right thing (there's a vast percentage more of do-gooders by the way)! So why not reward it to encourage it? Have you noticed that criminals are committing bigger and more extravagant crimes year after year? Ever wonder why? To get attention! To get their way! So as a society, let's start showing larger appreciation for doing a good thing. We can do that very easily by acknowledging our kids. If they open the door for someone, use their manners, give a hug or kiss just because (not at allowance time), we should reward them. If they ask how <u>your</u> day was and actually listened to your response (that would be a show stopper for sure), reward them! Let them go somewhere they've asked about, take them somewhere cool (<u>their</u> idea of cool), fork over some cash for that band they want to see, or just take them out to dinner at a nice restaurant. Whatever you need to do to say "thanks for being nice".

Household Contribution List (Chores) by Age

Toddler age 2-4

Fold laundry (pillowcases, bath towels, hand towels, washcloths)

Put dirty clothes in the hamper

Unload the dishwasher (low items-silverware, pots, and pans)

Put away toys

Dust

Swiffer the floor

Collect dirty clothes

Help transfer clothes from the washer to the dryer

Put clothes away in drawers

Make bed

Help put groceries away

Wipe cabinet doors*

Wipe baseboards *

Wipe countertops*

Stack pots in lower cabinets or drawers

Preschooler (ages 4-5)

All toddler chores

Load the dishwasher

Vacuum couch/ chairs/ cushions with handheld vacuum

Take out recycling

Set table

Clear table

Wash dishes (with supervision)

Clean windows

Wipe out bathroom sinks*

Vacuum floors (with a stick vac or handheld vacuum)

Match socks

Fold dish towels

Pull weeds

Harvest fruits and vegetables

Early Elementary (ages 6-8)

All toddler and preschool chores

<u>Meal prep</u> (wash produce, find ingredients, simple cutting-with plastic knife)

Wipe bathroom sinks, counters, scrub toilets*

Hang out laundry

Sweep

Vacuum

Collect garbage

Get mail

Fold/hang laundry

Clean microwave*

Rake leaves

Elementary (9-11)

All previous chores

Make simple meals

Take garbage/ recycling to the curb

Wash/ dry clothes

Clean toilets

Mop floors

Middle School (12-14)

Clean tub/ shower*

Make full meals/ meal plan

Clean out fridge/ freezer

Mow yard

Supervise younger children's chores

High School (15-18)

By this age, they should be able to do almost all chores without supervision. There are a few I'll throw in, like:

cleaning out the refrigerator*

cleaning out the garage

washing the cars

edging the lawn

small repairs

changing air filters in the house

running errands

doing the grocery shopping (by bike or car)

picking up prescriptions

taking the pet to vet appointments

taking siblings to appointments, practice or rehearsal

Of course, maturity and parental trust are huge factors for these lists and assigning chores should be taken into consideration on a case by case basis.

*I discovered an awesome cleaner online that gets our shower, tub, counters, cabinets, and even our spot cleaned carpets super clean! It's a mixture of blue dishwashing liquid (the one known to cut through grease), vinegar and water. Use an oz bottle and put 1 part dishwashing liquid to 2 parts vinegar. Fill with water and spray away! It is absolutely AWESOME, and even my husband is impressed with it (did I mention he's the original neat freak?) The vinegar is a natural cleaner and disinfectant, and the dishwashing liquid breaks up all kinds of gunk.

Basic Manners

This week I polled my kids on basic manners. I wanted to know what they thought basic manners were. When I asked my oldest son, he said, "Please, thank you, no ma'am, yes ma'am, no sir, yes sir, and be sure to introduce yourself". When asked what you could do with your body to show good manners, he was stumped. I had to throw him a bone. He came up with, "ladies first, don't talk with your mouth full (at least cover it if you have to talk), no yelling, no complaining, hold the door for everyone behind you" He also listed these as very important things to do: "take a shower, put on deodorant, and take all bodily functions to the bathroom". When I asked my daughter, she said: "respecting someone and not hurting their feelings." My middle child said nothing. He had a mouth full of snacks and waited until he had finished chewing. Then he said, "Saying can I be excused, saying excuse me when you burp, saying yes sir and yes ma'am, thank you and no thank you, yes sir and no sir, you're welcome, and that's all I can think of". I think they did a good job of covering the basics.

Other Important Parental Tools

You may want to download and browse the app, "urban dictionary" and do an internet search of "party games with drugs" or "weed party games", etc. Also, look for sites that give symptoms of drug use, games kids play at parties, or "how to take drugs, so your parents don't find out". While researching for this book, I found a site called marijuana.com. They give explicit details on how to use the drug. Why it's still there, I don't know. Hopefully, it's some trap to find people illegally using the drug. You can tell if your child is smoking by smelling their hair and fingers or by looking for burn marks on hands. You should also look for needle marks (I learned this trick teaching in public schools). You may even want to contact your local law enforcement to find out street names for drugs. You should always have a police officer or someone else in that arena to help you keep an eye out for trends that are out there. I have people in law enforcement, chemistry teachers, halfway house owners, and a ton of other people in my network, so I know what to look for to know the signs and symptoms of drug use.

Food Shouldn't Be a Reward

In former times, food was much less accessible, and using it as a reward was no big deal. My parents told me many stories about trips to get penny candy or soda when they got good grades or even how peaches from Papa's orchard was a rare treat. That was when food was cherished. Now there's so much food around it's unparalleled. Using food as a bribe ("clean your plate to get dessert") can set our kids up for physical failure later. Even using healthy foods as an incentive can be dangerous when given in excess.

I have many friends who admitted that they still operate under the house rules of "clean your plate before you get dessert", "we don't waste food in this house" and the notorious, "there are starving children in China/Africa." Let's do better by ourselves and by our kids. Coming up with alternatives such as going on a family trip, going to a new skate park, water park, or some other location may be a better way to inspire greatness and reward it as well.

7 TEENS (AND TWEENS)

Sneaking Out

Is your teen sneaking out of your house? There are different ways to address this problem. As a teen, I didn't think twice about sneaking out because there was a very clear consequence-the locks changed with me outside. They also let me know that the house came with the luxury of all items contained within: parents, food, clothing, my room, etc. So while my friends and relatives in other households snuck out to get drunk, high, and/or having sex, I was safely nestled in my room, considering the safety I was experiencing a blessing!

This section is meant for teens in high school, but I've read articles where children as young as 12 have snuck out of the house. This is not to be confused with running away, which is another topic. Running away is not addressed in this book.

One of the topics I researched for this book is children sneaking out while their parents are sleeping. There were many suggestions that I came across (most were legal) that I'd like to share. Again, I'm not a child counselor, therapist, or licensed professional on this topic, just a parent who found some ideas that may help you.

Before I jump into this subject, let me say this. The ease or difficulty of the teen years are usually predicated upon the caretaking of the earlier years (there are other factors as well). If you didn't listen, follow through, communicate clearly, have and maintain standards, or show sincere love and compassion, it can get very rough. Even if you've done all of those things, kids are kids. They want to experience what life is like outside of your parameters. Sometimes they'll feel the heat and drawback to safety. Sometimes they'll keep messing up until they get tired. Laying a good foundation is very, very important, but it won't keep your child from trying things.

Ok, on to the list of suggestions. If your child is sneaking out when you are asleep, consider these options (in no particular order and where applicable):

ASK- why are you sneaking out?

Put a Lojack on the car, phone, tablet, in their shoes, coat, book bag, or whatever they sneak out with.

Sleep in their room to deter their leaving

Catch them by sleeping in their room, and upon their return, talk to them about it.

If they're sneaking out to meet their boy/girlfriend, set up a meeting with <u>their</u> parents. You may want to set a meeting with the parents before confronting your child or their boy/girlfriend.

Set up a meeting with the boy/girlfriend and discuss what they're doing and why

Ground your child

Sign them up for community service during their "sneaking out hours" since they have <u>so</u> much energy

Talk to a probation officer for ideas

Install a door or window alarm (the magnetic/adhesive kind which sounds an alarm-not a hardwired system)

Show up where they are

Let your child know if you did the same thing when you were their age and have an honest discussion about the risks and the outcome (consider what it took for you to stop and try it with them. They are in fact, your child)

Let them know how it hurts your family

Discuss (<u>not yell</u>) your safety concerns. If you are thinking about loosening the reins and letting them go out, talk about security measures they should consider taking first.

Get a hard-wired alarm system in your house and put the control pad in your bedroom. Or get separate codes for kids and adults. You can get a text message or email if the alarm is disabled by anyone using a kid code.

Use a motion detection system in your house or motion-sensitive lighting outside your house (this works for people trying to sneak in or out!)

Monitor their social media accounts and/or cell phone to see what they're up to. You should always have access to their accounts and passwords. If they want access to use it, you should have access to it. If not, you may want to reconsider them having it. Same goes for cell phone and their codes. You should have access to that info if you're paying for them to access it (electric bill, internet bill, cell phone bill) or even if they're paying it (they're still staying in your house). Plus, it keeps everyone safe. See my tips on social media in the "Other things about going out…" section.

Actually, consider extending their curfew. I would only do this AFTER you give consequences for sneaking out and after <u>another 30-60 days minimum</u> of:

Not sneaking out

Abiding by all household rules

Fulfilling all obligations (for school, grades, chores, etc.)

Whatever else you deem necessary

One thing I've learned about parenting is that it requires research and trying new things. Don't shoot down an idea or practice of another parent if it actually works for their kid. Each person is an individual, and one size does not fit all.

Prom, Parties and Other Social Functions

I decided to speak specifically to this topic because I personally have a concern. Prom is great. Don't get me wrong. I enjoyed mine-responsibly. However, there were those who came back forever changed because of the choices they made. Be sure you know what your child will potentially experience when and if they go out prom night. It's not just the more basic sex, drinking, and weed that we remember-maybe you don't anymore. It's a slew of new, more potent prescription and non-prescription drugs (download urban dictionary to see a list of terms used), alcohol games you'd never imagine, new STDs, drunk driving, driving while texting and trying to post it on the fifty million social media sites available. You see on the news where adult lives are ruined because their lives were blasted for all the world to see.

Be sure to talk to your child about the importance of making good choices. One thing I can tell you is, when my parents didn't trust me to do the right thing (or hold up to the pressures of the atmosphere I wanted to enter into), they didn't let me go. Don't set your kid up for failure. If you know they're gonna do something stupid, why are you letting them go? But if you trust them, review the ground rules and let them experience a bit of life. Soapbox: My parents always said, "If you can't act like you have good sense at home, why would I let you out to act a fool in the street?"

The 5 Ws and an H System.

My parents used this and man, it worked! When I wanted to go somewhere, I'd have to answer those six questions. They went something like this:

Who are you going with? Who are you going to see?

Take notes on who they are leaving with and who they plan on meeting up with. Red flags should fly if it's someone you've never heard them mention before. It's really old school, but we as a culture need to revisit meeting the parents of our kid's friends at their house regularly.

What do you want to do? What will you be doing? What do you need?

Usually, kids aren't too shy about asking for cash. But, you need to know what you're funding. Don't give them too little, or they'll be put in a position to owe someone else a favor. Don't give them too much, or they could end up doing something crazy with it. Finally, if they get an allowance, make them use it! If they're bumming off you, make them work it off <u>before</u> you give it to them. This will also alleviate them not paying you back or springing an event on you. If they can't fund their endeavors, they don't need to go. You are not a walking ATM!

When are you leaving? When are you coming home? (this is a trick question, but sometimes they may come home before curfew)

Both questions are very important. Kids don't always leave when you are there with them. Sometimes they want to leave from school, from their bus stop, from your house, or from practice. You need to know when they are leaving because sometimes it tells you where they're leaving from. Also, let's face it. Teen brains aren't fully developed, and they don't always think things through. They are prone to leave out large pieces of important information like how they're getting there, the fact that they have some other function to attend, etc. Oh yeah, look out for these words: "Oh, I thought that you were gonna (take me, pick me up, pay, etc.)" Yeah, you're the parent when they want you to be and the warden when you have to be!

Where do you want to go? Do you have more than one destination?

Don't fall for a general answer for the first one. Sometimes more to it than what they're giving you. The second one is a setup. You must know if they plan on going just to the game or to the game, the mall, the movies, etc. I used to get into a ton of trouble when I was a kid because I didn't tell my parents all of the places I intended to go. I left them out purposely because I knew they'd say no. What's that saying? Oh yeah, the teen credo, "You are on a need to know basis." As parents, we have our own credo, "We need to know in case we have to save you!"

Why do you want to go? Why do they want you to go?

This one stumped me the first time I heard it. What do you mean, "Why do I want to go?" To get out of this house! DUH!! But it made me think about if I had a real purpose in going or if I was setting myself up to be in the wrong place at the wrong time. The second question really got me. Sometimes you know your friends are up to no good. You know they want you to get the car so they can proceed to get you in trouble. Yeah, we were all teenagers and had a friend who wanted you around to be their alibi.

Other Things About Going Out…

While I'm on this topic, I'd urge you to meet with a social media expert (or at least take a class if you're not versed in this sort of thing) so you can be sure you and your children have the proper settings on all of your social media sites. Be sure to check any devices that are connecting to the internet- even major appliances are even doing that now-so make sure they are secure. News articles are being released on how predators are finding people using the address on uploaded pics in email and social media. Be sure your GPS is turned off on your camera. Don't allow tracking for anything except your actual navigation app if you can help it. There are enough ways to get your personal info and whereabouts without we as citizens readily handing it over on a platter.

Finally, be sure to explain to your children that just because they delete an app from their phone doesn't mean the company doesn't still hold an account (and all of their information) on them. You must request to delete the account or unsubscribe from the service. But your info is still out there.

Parent Circle

If you're not already doing so, you need to stay in the parental loop. All kinds of crazy things (and good things) are going on with our kids, our neighborhoods, schools, and more that we need to be aware of. So get in some kind of group (not clique) where the focus is talking about our kids (not their parents, neighborhood gossip, etc.) Be sure to stay connected. Find out new and old info and share some yourself. All of our households will be stronger for it.

Sex

Yeesh. Who wants to talk to their kids about that?! Ok, to be fair, some parents dread it, and others are counting down to prepare their young ones. Experts said we should discuss sex with our children when they turn 12. The reasoning at that time was to not expose them to too much information before they needed it. Ha! Bogus. We started at age 10.

As I've mentioned before, I taught in several public schools. I taught 6th grade through adults. They come in the door knowing about sex. They know what it is, how to do it (most times they know more than adults), where to get it, what to call it. All some kids do is try to figure out who will do it and when. I had a student who had syphilis by the time she finished 6th grade. But the school board's stand was that students shouldn't be counseled in regards to sex (on any level- not even to tell them to wait) until they took sex Ed class, which was later in their education. Crazy, right? Well, you may disagree. To each his own. In any case, protect your child by giving them age and maturity appropriate information.

Recently, I participated in a mentoring program at our church, where I was given the lovely task of talking about sex. I had an audience of age 11-17. Tough crowd. Thank God I already knew all of them. But it was still rough. We opted to let the parents discuss it with the 11 and 12-year-olds that were present (I don't think they had a waiver to hear that portion), so we had mostly high schoolers.

One thing I wanted to be sure they knew was what to look for. People talk about the physical part of sex (the actual event), but when it comes to STDs, some things get left out. For instance, a yeast infection is not considered an STD, but it is spread mostly by sexual contact. It can even be spread by mouth. Not to mention that most men have no symptoms once they contract it and will continue to give it to their partner(s) even if she/they takes medication to cure it in her body. So the woman gets rid of it, engages with her partner again, and gets it again if he hasn't gotten rid of it.

We also had to talk about different visible symptoms in areas other than genitalia. It can be a very gross discussion, but you want them to know what they were looking at. It may look like a burst pimple on the mouth, but it could be something else. It could look like eczema or a basic rash or allergic reaction, but it could be something else. We have to educate our kids. Even if you don't want to get into it, you have to. If you don't know what to say, ask someone. At least do an internet search on the different STDs and let them look at the pictures. My Mom broke out a medical book with pictures of the STDs, and that locked me down for a long, long time. She told me, "Love yourself enough to keep yourself to yourself." I didn't understand at first, but I eventually did. I found out from watching others that I didn't to sign up for all the drama. They had to endure pressures of wearing a ton of makeup or certain clothes to impress a certain person, securing condoms or buying birth control, sneaking out to have sex, going to the clinic to get checked out, praying not to be pregnant or have an STD, etc. It also kept me from doing drugs and drinking (which usually was the setup for the sex the guys wanted to get out of you in the first place).

Work Together to Find Alternatives

Sometimes problems exist because kids have grown. They get bigger, their toys get bigger, their clothes get bigger. One indicator that you need to find a new storage system is a constantly messy room. My kids and I used to constantly battle over their messy rooms until I realized that they needed storage that fit them. Not just fit their stuff, but their organization styles. While those three drawer carts may work for one, shelves with smaller tubs work better for another. Bookshelves are great for some, but the way they are used may be far from their intended use. A dresser may work for some, but an armoire may work better for others. It may take trial and error or just asking. Find what works, implement it, and then hold them accountable.

This not only works for room organization but for learning styles as well. You may have been a night owl student, but your child could be an early bird. You may need absolute silence, but low playing music may help them focus. You may work great at a desk, but your child may excel while lying on the floor doing homework. Again, find what works and stick to it.

Are they always fighting over chores getting done? Let them pick their chore. If they choose the jobs that are way below their ability, who cares? Have them do two to three times the easy chores to compensate. Either way, the work is getting done, so don't knock it.

Boys

I should let my husband write this section. He is a genius. I have to admit it. For years and years, I've complained about the crazy stuff our oldest does and how he just doesn't get it. The child is not disobedient, but he doesn't get on the bus when it's at his stop all the time. You know, delayed obedience. He doesn't always realize that there's a window of time to get things done and that his delaying can disrupt the entire family. He's a tween trying to navigate the selfishness that occurs in those years. But, to stay on topic, my husband says that in all boys, there's a "click" when it all starts to come together. It's when they realize that the thing people have been trying to teach them was right. It depends on the boy, and it depends on their situation. It will occur almost at birth in some (the very serious child) to late thirties or forties for others (consider the movie Failure to Launch). When the "click" occurs, they'll start cleaning up without being told, actually washing properly and having more of a team mindset. I am happy to report that the "click" has not occurred for my first son yet, but he is showing tendencies. So, there is hope! But as for your household, what would I suggest? PATIENCE. Lots and lots of patience. Keep sowing those seeds of instruction without "losing it" and wait for the "click".

Other "Boy Tips"

Avoid walking into their room at night with no light on.

If you walk into the room at night with no light on, walk like you are skiing (slide your feet across the floor) very slowly. You'll avoid stepping on dinosaurs, joysticks, or other random items.

Do not ever, ever, ever smell their laundry once they've begun to smell like boys. EVER. Did I mention EVER? When they begin to smell like boys, make them smell their own laundry or just wash it all. It's not worth the risk of the mental help required afterward.

If your son tries to sneak and play video games at night, flip his breaker to his room. His lights will still work (in most houses), but he won't be up at all hours trying to play games or watch TV. If he has an HDTV, confiscate the cord every night. You can also put a tiny lock (like we girls used on our diaries back in the day) through the TV plug. Another option? Have him check out his joysticks every day and return them at bedtime.

Post the morning routine (wash face, brush teeth, comb hair, put on deodorant) on their bathroom mirror inside a clear sleeve. Hang it with the open side down or tape it closed. This will keep water from leaking in. It sounds weird, but trust me. Hang it upside down.

Let Them Hit the Wall

Let's define "hitting the wall". The more widely used definition is when you keep making the same mistake over and over and don't plan on ever-changing your behavior because no consequence has been big enough to make you change your habits. When you hit the wall, you have no more options. You have to face your mess, deal with it, and then move on. This is the "hitting the wall" that is a result of your own personal decisions. There's another type of hitting the wall, though.

Hitting the wall is also when you are going along, doing well, and all of a sudden, you're faced with a challenge in life that is too high to get over, too wide to get around, and too hard to go through. For boys, they will (in some cases, not all) stand at the wall and linger there even though they'll see others overcome it easily. My husband described it this way:

A boy is standing in front of a wall. He has been there for a long time. A small, young girl comes to the wall. She says hello and begins to ask him questions. She asks, "How long have you been here?" He says, "A while", even though it's really been a long time. She asks, "Do you need some help?" He says in a cocky tone, "No, I got this." She asks, "How did you get the bruises and scars on your hands?" He replies, "From trying to go through this wall." She nods and then asks, "What are you waiting for?" He responds, "I'm resting up so I can try to go through this wall again." She nods, backs up, and surveys the wall. She turns around and walks away. She returns shortly with a ladder. She leans it on the wall, climbs up the ladder, and goes over the wall. The ladder remains. So does the boy. He looks at the ladder and the path the girl took. He takes a deep breath and preps himself to punch through the wall again.

Boys can be like this sometimes. They are sometimes taught that it's nobler to be tough than to be considered a thinker. So even in simple situations, they try to make their own way instead of using the resources right in front of them. There are also some boys who will stand at the wall and wait for someone to bring a ladder they can use instead of getting their own. There will come a point, though, when they must make it on their own. So, if your son has hit the wall, he has to decide three things: How long do I stay here? How do I get to the other side? Do I want to get to the other side?

"The wall" can be many things. It can be large or small decisions such as doing homework or chores, a peer pressure situation, or exploring a new career path. They may need to be reminded they have options, what they are, and may need help figuring out their next move.

When my husband and I talk about our sons, we often discuss the wall. As parents, we are often on different sides of the wall. I'm on the Mom side, and he's on the Dad side. I'm giving warnings, counsel (wanted and unwanted), and anything else I can throw in there to keep him from hitting the wall. Dad? Let him hit it. He's gotta be a man. He'll be fine. Now, I used to argue about it and try to help the boy. Lately, not so much. My husband is right. He's gotta hit the wall to realize that it is real. It will not just up and move for you, and you have to live your life. At this stage in my son's life, it's more about doing chores and homework. Later it'll be about some girl, finding an apartment, getting a degree, or getting a job. I can't baby him. He has to grow up, and I have to let him. But if he needs me, I mean *really* needs me, I'll always be there! So I'll step back and let others mentor him, let him have valuable life experiences, and when he decides to, let him bump his head on that wall until he's motivated enough to get himself to the other side.

Other issues? Value. If boys don't know their value, they fall into traps of peer pressure. They'll feel the need to impress, outdo, and exceed just to feel loved and wanted. When they don't feel that consistently, you'll see gravitation toward people and activities that cause damage to their mind, bodies, and their future. That's why it's important to give a good balance of positive reinforcement and correction. Too much positive reinforcement can lead to a lazy bones, an individual with low standards or expectations, or an all-out spoiled brat. Too much correction can lead to a crushed spirit, him being a people pleaser, a perfectionist, a workaholic, or worse. I hate to bring it up, but it seems that we have more young men committing suicide in this generation than I ever remember. There's got to be a reason. Let's think about what those reasons could be. Are we creating balanced sons? Do they know we love them for them and not for what they do or can become?

Girls

In my observation, daughters can navigate walls without much problem. Little girls are taught to observe, evaluate, think, strategize, whatever you want to call it. Don't get me wrong. They may have a few walls that they will seem to camp out in front of, However, it appears to me that those are not the heavy hitters. It's the <u>MIRRORS</u> that are the danger for our girls! For whatever reason, it seems to take a lot of time for women to figure out who they are, accept who they are, and decide to love themselves. We have to get past the "too _____" (ugly, fat, skinny, tall, short, smart, loud…) traps and get to the place of peace with who we are. If more young ladies were taught their own value instead of comparing themselves to someone else, would be fewer occurrences of teenage suicide, self-abuse, pregnancy, STDs, and a myriad of other problems our society faces.

How do you help these young ladies? Validation. Especially by fathers. My husband actually calls my daughter "princess", "beautiful", "smart", etc. so when some guy comes along and tells her that she won't be floored by a decent compliment and run off with him. Dads, take your daughter out to dinner, the movies, or a Daddy-daughter getaway to <u>nice</u> places. Take her with you places so she can see how a lady is to be treated. Show her examples of what you do and don't want her to do. Sometimes my daughter and husband will be walking together, and he'll say, "Baby, please don't ever dress like she's dressed. It'd make Daddy sad." She takes that to heart.

My daughter was taught at an early age that anything above the knee wasn't appropriate unless she was in a room by herself. Now she won't wear short skirts, "booty shorts" or anything that shows too much. She goes to her father to see if every new garment meets his approval. I'm proud to say that I taught her to go to him, first thing. She even puts my clothes in place if something is getting too revealing. She says, "Ooooh. Mommy, you're showing too much."

Then she turns her head away, closes her eyes, and then reaches out to put whatever it is in the right place. I love how she cares enough to "defend my honor" when I'm unaware that my clothes are out of place!

Moms, take time to teach your daughter how to be a lady. This could mean a number of things to you. It could be how to value yourself or love yourself. It may be place settings, how to get in and out of a car properly, how to wear makeup, do your nails, hair salon etiquette, how to walk in heels, types of people to avoid, or whatever! Whatever valued lessons you want her to learn, start early. If you don't start early, at least start. Set a bar for them (that's within reach with a bit of stretching) and celebrate their progress.

Long story short, kids need their parents to encourage and validate them. They want what we all want. Love. Respect. Room to just "be". Affection. Kindness. Tenderness. Understanding. Let's get to it. Their lives are at stake!

Keep Them Around "Normal" a Lot

I know that sounds like a crazy statement, but what it means is this-when children (or anyone, really) is around correct behavior enough, the incorrect behavior looks and feels wrong. My pastor says, "You are who you hang around." My parents always said, "Birds of a feather flock together." So if you want your child to behave a certain way, put them in circles of that behavior. If your child comes home from school acting like a world-class jerk, you can talk to them about it, get the teacher to move their seat or change their class. If your child comes home smelling like smoke, alcohol, or weed, do something about it! Change their circles. You have the power. You'll have to wield it like a sword until they can do battle for themselves. Hang in there!

Don't Stop Teaching!

Even though we start early, we have to keep pounding that drum (constantly teaching) through adulthood. Their age may change, but the overall issues are still the same. Once a parent always a parent, I've heard. Many parents I've interviewed say it's much harder being a parent of adult children than of little ones! You know how you watch a movie or game on TV, and you already know what's gonna happen, so you're shouting warnings or plays at the TV, but they don't listen? Yeah, that's adult parenthood. As they grow older into adults, they aren't required to listen to you on the level that they were before. This leaves parents on the outside of the game looking in. When you have less and less control over their decisions, instead of being a teacher, you become more of a consultant and a role model. This is where the pain of parenthood really kicks in. This is the part of their life where you see the trap laid, you give warnings, you are not being listened to, and experience the pain of seeing your child suffer. But that's life. They have to be allowed to make their own decisions, navigate around obstacles, and find their way out of pits. They are stronger for it, and that is our job as parents to provide them with the tools they need to navigate life.

As my kids grow and I compare them to myself (yeah, I do, but I don't tell them that), I see the importance of playing mentally stimulating games. I don't like how much my kids adore video games. However, I must admit that playing a million games on those old school game systems did a great deal for my hand-eye coordination, problem-solving skills, tenacity (man it took forever to win some of them!), self-esteem and logic skills. I also realize that playing board games, word finds, puzzles, and building block systems did a great deal for those same skills. And nothing can beat a good cardboard box, making mud pies, building forts with sheets, playing with clay or log building sets! That doesn't even scratch the surface. Man, we had fun when we were kids!

I talk to my students (I still teach math sometimes) about their college experience versus mine. I tell them they don't get it. There's no way they can recapture or completely understand or experience the culture we had. There were not many with cars on campus, so we came up with things to do in the dorms. College campuses now are ghost towns on the weekends. Either everyone is holed up in their room with a gadget, or they skip town. No late-night parties, card games, trying out hairdos (and hair don'ts), trash-talking with friends, walking across campus for late meals, or just sitting outside hanging out. We only had about five channels (no cable), so unless you were gonna watch an 80-year-old lawyer in a seersucker suit or some urban sitcoms based on college, you were out of luck. It pushed us to connect on a deeper level. We knew who people were because we spent time with them. It wasn't this pseudo-connection mess they have now where you can create an alternate personality digitally. People were in your personal space and interacted with you, so they could see who you really were!

However, I have to be fair. On the other side of the coin, I must say that the kids now have the entire world at their fingertips. While we were limited in the cultures we could experience, the kids now can meet with people from all over the world. I have experienced it and love it! I've recently met people I would never have met due to the services our business uses. I have YouTube followers and Facebook fans that span the globe! It's awesome to know that you have the ability to make an impact on the world. We must make sure we teach our kids to use this power responsibly and not corrupt it with selfies of inappropriate, degrading material, but enlightening contributions that will make the world a better place. So parents, never stop teaching. Teach your kids, the neighbor's kids, community kids, the world's kids. We can only reap a huge reward in the end.

ABOUT THE AUTHOR

Tonya E. Joyner is a wife, mother of three, book publisher, speaker, author, educator, trainer, and entrepreneur. She's loved and taught children and adults for over 25 years. Out of that love, she authored this book and her first book, *Mostly Sunny…With a Chance of Clouds & Rain.* Her current books are available in print, on Amazon.com and also available on Kindle. She also opened her own book publishing company, TJS Publishing House. Find the solution to all of your self-publishing and traditional publishing needs at www.tonyajoyner.com.

Printed in Great Britain
by Amazon

43629545R00078